A-BUN-DANCE
4 YOUR FINANCE

Growing Interest About Money
Even if you Have ADHD

ZARINA BOILY

BALBOA.PRESS
A DIVISION OF HAY HOUSE

Copyright © 2019 Zarina Boily.

All rights reserved. No part of this book may be used or reproduced by any means, graphic, electronic, or mechanical, including photocopying, recording, taping or by any information storage retrieval system without the written permission of the author except in the case of brief quotations embodied in critical articles and reviews.

Balboa Press books may be ordered through booksellers or by contacting:

Balboa Press
A Division of Hay House
1663 Liberty Drive
Bloomington, IN 47403
www.balboapress.com
844-682-1282

Because of the dynamic nature of the Internet, any web addresses or links contained in this book may have changed since publication and may no longer be valid. The views expressed in this work are solely those of the author and do not necessarily reflect the views of the publisher, and the publisher hereby disclaims any responsibility for them.

The author of this book does not dispense medical advice or prescribe the use of any technique as a form of treatment for physical, emotional, or medical problems without the advice of a physician, either directly or indirectly. The intent of the author is only to offer information of a general nature to help you in your quest for emotional and spiritual well-being. In the event you use any of the information in this book for yourself, which is your constitutional right, the author and the publisher assume no responsibility for your actions.

Any people depicted in stock imagery provided by Getty Images are models, and such images are being used for illustrative purposes only. Certain stock imagery © Getty Images.

Print information available on the last page.

ISBN: 978-1-9822-5445-2 (sc)
ISBN: 978-1-9822-5447-6 (hc)
ISBN: 978-1-9822-5446-9 (e)

Library of Congress Control Number: 2020917052

Balboa Press rev. date: 12/15/2020

CONTENTS

Introduction
A Journey Begins vii

Chapter 1
Where No One Has Gone Before 1

Chapter 2
Only You Can Choose to Create a New Life 21

Chapter 3
When Integrity and Finances Collide 47

Chapter 4
Acknowledge the Situation, and Embrace Change 65

Chapter 5
Assess Your Relationship with Money 79

Chapter 6
Know Where Your Cash Flows 91

Chapter 7
Finances, Self-Worth, and Nutrition 103

Chapter 8
Be Account-*Able* 127

Chapter 9
Money as a Sacred Partner 141

INTRODUCTION
A Journey Begins

Create the space and a
bigger life happens.
-Alysia Reiner

Nature *is* abundant. There are countless trees, branches, and leaves. Some have beautiful flowers that spread a pleasant perfume or produce delicious fruits. Others have pines. Nature is an abundant green oasis that brings a calm and peaceful feeling.

Green is also the color of the heart chakra, healing, and manifestation. What I know to be true is that each lesson learned brings deep awareness to your being and takes part in your healing process.

Winds are blowing strong. A few clouds are suspended in the sky, flowing peacefully.

A Journey Begins

Have you ever taken the time to stop and admire the beauty all around you while enjoying a quiet moment in nature?

Maybe you have experienced a deep, strong sense of abundance by doing so, but if you haven't, it truly is an incredible feeling. Spending time outdoors—whether it's a walk in the forest, standing by the ocean looking at the infinite horizon, gardening, or any activity that frees your spirit sending it into a calm state of mind—is a perfect way to practice being completely present.

Show presence with your surroundings as you take time to yourself.

Show presence by being aware of your body and how it occupies space in each new environment you inhabit.

Show presence with each of your senses. View the scenery while the trees and leaves dance to the rhythm of the wind. Listen to the birds sing while you feel the warmth of the sun and the cool breeze touch your skin. Inhale the powerful smells of the wildflowers.

Show presence by opening your heart to all the greatness and beauty that surrounds you, allowing yourself to be receptive, in sync with the world around you, as it is a representation of what is waiting to be discovered right inside of you. Feel the love.

Immersed in this moment, you may realize that life is abundant, and so are we since we are one with everything that is.

While on your quest, you may be searching for answers and trying to find them in the wrong places. Until you become aware that what you see outside of you comes from within you, it may be a never-ending search.

Making Each Day Count

Passing through life and dancing with life are two very different things. The second one allows us to see that abundance takes many forms, and one of them is life itself.

Once you realize all that is abundant around you and reinforce your connection to the fantastic and nourishing beauty available to you, chances are you will see more of what Source has provided for you to strive.

Another amazing thing resides in this principle: abundance is something that begins within.

For instance, look at the physical body. There are billions of cells working together in complex ways, 24-7.

Cells alone are a microscopic form of abundance, don't you think?

A Journey Begins

Unfortunately, the ego plays its role well in fooling us, so we believe we are not enough or are undeserving and unworthy. Bit by bit, our connection to the divine (the universe or whatever you call it) is lost, and parts of ourselves forgotten.

While growing up, it always felt weird to me and didn't make sense that life was composed of three stages. There is so much more to life than coming into this world, living, and dying.

Our goal as humans is to grow on many different levels so that ultimately, we can be whole and can live and shine in our essence where love, peace, enlightenment, abundance, and harmony prevail.

How do you get to that profound feeling of connection with everything, and what does it have to do with financial abundance?

Engraved in your cells, DNA, and subconscious lies information that influences how you think, feel, and act, as well as what you believe and how you have built your relationship with money. If you happen to be struggling with managing your finances, chances are there are some cleaning and clearing to do.

The healing process will take you on many avenues that may unearth unpleasant emotions, thoughts, and feelings. These newly discovered artifacts may show up as frustration, dissatisfaction, or lack of faith because you feel limited on your quest for abundance. Deconstructing limiting beliefs that don't serve you anymore and replacing them with new, positive ones leads you to build self-esteem and self-worth, loving yourself, and being able to ask for and receive help when needed. This process will peel off layers that ultimately bring you closer to your true self and open the door to greater abundance.

Finance and Money—A Pain in the Brain When You Have ADHD

If you are living with ADHD, does any of the following sound familiar? Managing money is challenging and overwhelming. Paying bills on time is something you don't often experience as opposed to spending impulsively. Finding that your debt keeps piling up, misplacing money from your wallet, borrowing money, or even trying to stick to a budget without pulling your hair are situations you find yourself in regularly. How about consolidating debt to lower the interest you are losing to the bank and finding yourself in the same situation a few years later.

Hey! I know the feeling. I've been where you are, trying to master the art of financial health and financial intelligence, feeling overwhelmed and asking myself questions I didn't have answers to—feeling anxious, stressed, and so insecure about money until

A Journey Begins

Before revealing the turning point that helped turn things around, allow me to share a glimpse of my financial heritage.

For both my parents, money was a great source of stress and worries. My mother lived with the fear and insecurity of not having enough and wondered how they would make it from the moment they knew I was coming.

Those worries, stresses, and fears about money were the same for their parents, and grandparents and went back twelve generations of ancestors before me.

Abundance also manifests at the cellular level. What follows might be a stretch, but you already are a trillionaire because you have an estimated number of cells in the human body is 30 trillion or 30,000,000,000,000!

Talking about cells, DNA, and subconscious programming, I guess my memory and hard drive were full!

Everything I experienced from my mother about money as a child created my belief systems around abundance. I assume it was the same way for everyone.

What I perceived as a child created one souvenir in particular that remained engraved in my head for the longest time. Watching my mother counting out all of her earnings to make sure she had enough to provide for our basic needs and her financial responsibilities and it actually is a good thing. She always paid her bills on time. However as a young sensitive and intuitive girl, I was feeling her fear of lack without knowing it.

As a single mother (or any parent), she prioritized survival and worked hard to ensure we had a roof over our heads, food on the table, and clothes to wear.

We always had everything we needed, and she even bought a house near my grandparents, where we would go for a summer vacation. This achievement ignited such a profound sense of pride for her. I'll never forget it.

I don't remember having the feeling we were poor or less fortunate. I remember thinking how unfair it was that some had more money than others. I wondered why it was that way, why we didn't have more.

One day as I watched my mother at the kitchen table, counting her money again, I decided I would *never* spend my life counting mine. Can you see the belief system taking form?

Nope.

Rather than saving it, money, to me, existed to be spent. I couldn't have cared less about where my

A Journey Begins

cash went or what I spent it on. If I wanted something, I wouldn't think twice and buy it instead of paying my phone bill.

I was determined to control money instead of allowing it to control me as I believed it controlled my mother.

As Simba in the movie *The Lion King* laughed in the face of danger, I laughed in the face of money.

It was foolish even to think of controlling money as possible. Fortunately, things have evolved.

Along with the family heritage came a brain wired differently, with a disinterest in money management. Forty years of my life went by without me knowing this fact about myself or explaining part of my unhealthy relationship with money.

I am not a fan of the boxes our society creates for people. For example, I prefer referring to myself as an *Indigo* rather than a woman with ADHD, and acquiring a better understanding of my uniquely wired brain was remarkably helpful. When you don't know how your engine works, it's hard or nearly impossible to move forward. It feels like learning to drive a standard car, waiting at a red light uphill, and finding the right balance between the clutch and the gas pedal, so it doesn't go downhill.

If you have heard the term "*Indigo*," you know that these children and adults have characteristics that are almost identical to certain ADHD traits. Their presence on earth is needed to create and help humanity awaken spiritually.

Indigos are gifted and known to be freethinkers. They also find it hard to adapt and fit into our society, mainly because they feel and see what the mainstream doesn't or ignores.

As individuals with the ability to know what's real and what's not, you can say they have a sixth sense or a bullshit detector that's undeniable. Often misunderstood, rejected, or misdiagnosed with ADD or ADHD, their intuition is powerful. You may recognize yourself as being *Indigo* if the following describes you:

- strong-willed
- struggles with boredom
- considered an old soul
- a freethinker
- nonconformist
- perceptive and intelligent
- highly intuitive
- empathetic and compassionate
- highly creative
- more sensitive to environmental and food pollutants

You may also have spiritual gifts, such as clairvoyance or telepathy, and a profound connection with animals and nature.

Finding Meaning

Things need to make sense and have a purpose for indigos; otherwise, the same behavior—whether it be procrastination, uncontrolled spending, or lack of discipline in managing finances—will be repeated indefinitely. Here are a few things that are getting in the way:

- your system of limiting beliefs
- your family heritage
- your disinterest in finances because it can cause overwhelm
- your ego
- your low self-awareness

What does it keep you from being, doing, and having? Keep on reading. You'll find out soon enough!

Now back to that extraordinary brain.

The moment I discovered what I much prefer calling a difference than a disorder, a strong impulse took over my entire body. Something inside came alive. Right there and then, it became crystal clear that I wanted to help others embrace their uniqueness, their highly creative genius, and their strengths.

Life has this magical way of speaking to you and does so in many forms. Slowing down and practicing to listen is a must to hear, see, and feel those exact messages.

The Journey Is the Destination

When you choose to walk on the path of personal growth, you may, at times, feel as if you are moving forward at the pace of a sea turtle coming out of the ocean, making her way slowly in the sand until it can finally rest.

You may believe there is a destination to be reached. However, personal transformation and spiritual growth are not things you buy a plane ticket to—get there quickly. Your journey is your destination.

There is often a pivotal moment, or a succession of events you can refer to, as to when it all begins. I was unaware of it then, but mine was in September 2007.

At the time, my journalism career was stressful and extremely demanding as the television station I worked for had reduced the department's budget to cut down expenses. I was doing three jobs: reporter, camerawoman, and editor of my TV news reports.

A Journey Begins

To make a long story short, I began experiencing built-up frustration, and I lacked any kind of motivation. My body was sending me messages I kept ignoring, unaware of the physical damages and the emotional and psychological imbalances it was causing.

Fortunately, a friend I had lost track of reached out one day, and our conversation led to the importance of providing our body with the best nutrition possible. To this day, I consider this moment a divine intervention because it led to leading a more fulfilling life.

When your cells lack vital nutrients, your body can hardly keep accomplishing the thousands of functions it needs to perform at an optimal level. In my case, the nutrient deficiency was so high that even though I was taking top-quality supplements to fill in the gap, the damages caused by the tremendous amount of stress I was under hadn't prevented me from burning out.

Perfectionism and unworthiness, which are common with ADHD, are the significant factors that led to a one-year leave of absence from work in 2008.

And strangely enough, passion for physical, emotional, and psychological health emerged in the following year, which opened the pathway to the beginning of my spiritual awakening.

Numerology has been a great way to find exciting things about myself and a fun way to play with numbers.

The year 2019 marked the beginning of a nine-year cycle for me. I pulled the plug on my journalism career in 2009! I can't believe how time flies!

Celebration time! (By the way, this book gives you plenty of opportunities to celebrate as you read!)

I wish to celebrate my tireless determination, incredible resilience, and genius—or my zone of excellence if you prefer. There have been many ups and downs, but they have contributed to my tremendous growth. Even though there were times when I thought of giving up, I am glad I didn't. I am incredibly proud of what I've put in place to increase my interest in finances.

Your turn now! Take a few minutes. Close your eyes, breathe deeply and slowly, and reflect on what you've read so far.

How do you feel?
_____
_____
_____
_____

Does it stir any emotions? Which ones?
_____
_____
_____
_____

A Journey Begins

What can you celebrate at this moment?

_____
_____
_____
_____

Writing this book is the perfect way to honor and celebrate this chapter of my life. Countless lessons have brought valuable awareness, beautiful experiences, and a lot of tears and resistance from my ego, which translated into physical aches.

There were numerous moments of grace, including a massive opening of the heart after finding my way back to God—or, as I said before, any other name you use, in respect of what you believe.

All of our lives have ups and downs. It is how we learn. What matters in a situation or experience isn't the situation or experience itself but how you perceive it and react to it. There is no need to stay in emotional turmoil or resist change. The only one that benefits from that is your ego. Convincing yourself that it is a form of protection will only make things a lot worse.

We don't need to lead our lives with ego, but we sure need to redefine its role. In this present time, we also need to find the key to unlock the suffering built up in our hearts and open them wide to heal and receive love in the purest, most Divine way.

Suffering, getting sick, and wanting to crawl out of your skin is optional.

A-Bun-Dance 4 Your Finance is meant to help you move forward and bring enthusiasm, simplicity, and cohesion to help you grow interested in managing your money. It links together things that seem opposed at first—like money, nutrition, and self-worth—but that ends up making sense.

A-Bun-Dance 4 Your Finance is also meant to be fun as playfulness is a significant value for *Indigo* individuals. Fun sparks interest, which ignites attention and fires up the ability to focus.

Read this book with an open mind and heart. Be willing to experience new things and see this book as an adventure. Feel free to tweak the exercises if you sense that works best for you. It's okay if you don't agree with everything I share. Honor your journey.

The teachings in this book come from the road I've been on to transition from having no interest whatsoever in money, refusing to let it control me because I hated it to transforming the love-hate relationship I had with it. Now I appreciate money greatly and consider it an incredible ally.

Deep in my soul, I know this book will allow for great liberation, healing, and laughter. There might be tears as well, and that, too, is part of the process.

A Journey Begins

However, it's okay if some of the content doesn't resonate with you right now, that's okay. You can always revisit it later.

Authenticity is a value I cherish, and *A-Bun-Dance 4 Your Finance* will give you exactly that. No sugarcoating. I tell it as it is—the good, the bad, and the not so pretty.

The more authentic and truthful you are in doing the exercises, the more you will gain from them. You may not have all the answers right away, but don't worry; eventually, you will find them. Make sure you stick a Post-it or a fun sticker beside it so you can easily see it as you flip through the book.

Always have a pen or pencil. I like to use a pencil and an eraser because I tend to get distracted when what I write isn't neat. You can also carry a notebook or journal as insights, answers and questions may come when you least expect them.

Writing them down will prevent you from forgetting valuable information, especially with a brain operating at the speed of light.

With this book comes the hope that you will begin a meaningful journey of self-discovery, with greater awareness about how, when, and why you manage, spend, and care for money the way you do.

- May your growing interest in money management set a positive example for your kids as they learn from what they see you doing.
- May your assertiveness, self-worth, and mindfulness increase to a whole new level.
- May you have a blast through the process

A-Bun-Dance 4 Your Finance is your coach on paper with a simple but genuine intention. I designed these tools to help you and be a support system for you by uniting my strong desire to guide you to ultimate financial success with my passion for writing—a gift to you from someone who truly understands the difficulty of silencing negative thoughts.

It's like using a GPS. Without an address, it's impossible to get anywhere. This book is part of an itinerary on the road to abundance in all forms, since important components are part of it, as you will discover in the following chapters.

Reading this book shows you have the desire to improve your financial situation and are willing to roll up your sleeves and do the work honestly and transparently as you start your journey to a-bun-dance.

You will see these four graphics throughout the book. These graphics are meant to make your learning experience and processing of the information ADD friendly so you can easily focus, pay attention, and grow your interest in managing your money.

A Journey Begins

(Notebook) This design invites you to take a moment to answer questions, writing down your thoughts, or any questions that might arise. This activity helps you reflect and answer the tough questions of life to help you move forward. It also is a safe space to externalize whatever needs to come out.

(Gold bar) When you see this image it is time to get down to business as it indicates a finance exercise. For example, you might have to do a money investigation to determine where the leaks are so you can stop them.

(Key) The key is a symbol you will use to unlock or uncover limiting beliefs you need to let go of, stories you tell yourself that are erroneous and keep you from the incredible treasures awaiting discovery. It creates a clearer understanding of who you truly are and allows for self-discovery.

(Diamond) The diamond indicates that it is time to celebrate. It also means start shaping something new, unique, and magnificent, just like you. Write down your dreams, and dream big. Feel it. Smell it. Hear it. See it. Touch it. Speak it. Taste it.

How can you sparkle more?

What makes you shine brightly?

A New Perspective on Money for People with ADHD

It is my most deep-rooted belief that I was able to go from no interest in finances to annual financial planning and enjoying playing with a budget, anyone can.

Our brains are uniquely wired, and we need to stop working against them and learn how to work with them. So, here's a quick overview of what this book offers.

You will:

- find out which traits interfere with your ability to manage money,
- grow interest in your finances,
- identify and stop financial leaks,
- a shift from being overwhelmed by money controlling you to being empowered by managing it wisely,
- experience peace of mind and heart, and
- have a variety of simple tools and exercises to guide you.

You won't:

- find tedious technical and scientific data on how and why ADHD comes with a challenge in managing money,
- come across tools and strategies that only make you work on the surface,

- get a quick fix, or
- have any guarantee of the results you will get—because that, my dear, is up to you and how badly you want things to improve.

Before you go on, here are a few facts about ADHD and money. This is as technical as I am going to get, as I believe it is part of the challenge, not an entirety.

Lack of impulse control can lead to unnecessary spending. It is the inability to manage or modulate emotions or reactions. Boredom is something that can ignite impulsivity.

Weak follow-through and time insensitivity can also hinder your ability to manage money well.

Engaging our brain to keep persevering and to finish something we started seems like running a marathon. Sprinting suits us better as it is short and sweet. Not having any sense of time explains late bill payments as well as lack of interest.

On a scale of 1 to 10 (1 being not at all and ten being very much), what level do you recognize yourself? (Circle the corresponding number).

1 2 3 4 5 6 7 8 9 10

- large or small purchases that you end up regretting (not to be mistaken with manic spending)
- inability to stick to a budget or to track mentally how a purchase fits in the bigger picture
- uncontrolled spending, such as unneeded and unwanted things you can't afford and feel ashamed or embarrassed afterward
- black-and-white/all-or-nothing thinking

It is important to know where you are now to make changes last. Then you take one step forward and another one and so on.

The following questionnaire helps you assess your financial situation as of today.

Don't be discouraged or overwhelmed about the situation.

Remember: what matters in a situation or experience isn't the situation or experience itself but how you perceive, react to it, and act on it.

Ask yourself, "What can I do to improve the situation?"

This book will provide tips to help you do it.

Focus on solutions rather than what you don't have because the fear of lack will only bring you more lack.

A Journey Begins

The intention behind the questions below is to help you start drawing an accurate portrait of your financial situation.

Collecting data is crucial as what's bound to happen is you become aware of numbers that can't be ignored forever—not if you wish to experience financial freedom in this lifetime.

As you do this exercise, put aside any judgment, criticism, self-blame, shame, or anger. When you're done, use the space provided to write down your thoughts, emotions, and feelings.

ADHD and Money Questionnaire

(Gold bar) When something stinks, you can either ignore the smell or put your nose in it to find out where it's coming from so you can fix it. The more aware you are of a situation, the better. Answer the following questions by checking *yes* or *no*.

		Yes	No
1	Do you often make purchases on impulse?		
2	Are your credit cards full or over the limit?		
3	Do you know your debt ratio?		
4	Have you ever had bad credit?		
5	Do you have savings?		

A-BUN-DANCE 4 YOUR FINANCE

6	Do you often pay your bills, loans, and other financial obligations late or not at all because you forget?		
7	Do you have a retirement savings plan?		
8	Do you have financial goals?		
9	When you pay with checks, do they bounce most of the time?		
10	Do you lose receipts or other important documents for income taxes?		
11	Have you lost friends after not paying back the money you borrowed from them?		
12	Do you get late fees for unpaid bills?		
13	Do you know where to find important documents?		
14	Is your credit rating poor because of late payments or defaulting on loans?		
15	Do you know the balance of your bank accounts?		
16	Is making a minimum payment on your credit card difficult?		
17	Has poor money management ever made you consider filing for, or have you filed for bankruptcy?		
18	Do you balance your checkbook regularly?		
19	Is money or lack of financial management a source of conflict with your partner or spouse?		
20	Do you receive overdue payment notices often?		
21	Do you have a personal/family budget?		

A Journey Begins

22	If you have a personal/family budget, do you stick to it?		
23	Do you know how much interest you pay per year on credit cards, loans, and mortgages?		
24	Do you know the interest rates of your credit cards, loans, and mortgages?		
25	Have you ever worked with, or consider working with, a financial planner?		
26	Do you have money saved for emergencies or something unexpected like a car repair, a new pair of glasses, or dental care?		
27	If you were forced to stop working or lost your job, would you have enough money saved to cover three to six months of your expenses?		
28	Do you feel overwhelmed by the tasks to be accomplished in money management?		
29	Do you procrastinate paying your bills?		
30	Are you aware of your spending behaviors and habits?		
31	Do you have difficulty prioritizing, organizing, and making decisions when it comes to money?		
32	Can you differentiate luxury from necessity?		
33	Do you live from paycheck to paycheck?		
34	Do you misplace money from your wallet?		

What are your thoughts after completing the questionnaire?

What emotions does it bring up?

What feeling?

Write them down:

_____
_____
_____
_____

Using a scale of 1 to 10 (1 being little or no interest and 10 being totally interested in money and financial management), at what level are you? (Circle the corresponding number.)

1   2   3   4   5   6   7   8   9   10

Feeling Celebratory?

(Diamond) A celebration is a crucial factor in helping anchor something positive. As one of the challenges with ADHD is having difficulty being aware of the world inside, it is essential to create a system of elements for reference. This is a great way to shift focus and pay attention to what you do well, excel in, and where you have talent. As a bonus, it opens the door to gratitude.

A Journey Begins

Now, what can you celebrate?
_____
_____
_____
_____

What are you proud of?
_____
_____
_____
_____

Any new awareness?
_____
_____
_____
_____

What was your aha moment (a sudden insight or realization of something becoming crystal clear)?
_____
_____
_____
_____

Friendly Reminders for A-Bun-Dance 4 Your Finance

1. Invest in spending time in nature to connect to all its abundance.

2. Your outside world is a reflection of your inside world. Chaos comes from within, as does personal peace.

3. Each lesson learned brings deep awareness and is part of your healing process.

4. Finding meaning helps you increase your interest in finance and money and reduces brain aches.

5. Healing your relationship with money sets a solid foundation for your kids.

6. Focus on solutions rather than problems or what you don't have because the fear of lack will only bring you more of both.

7. Keep an open mind to create a new perspective on money.

8. Loss of presence and fun are two powerful indicators that your interest is decreasing. Remember the reasons you decided to go on this journey.

CHAPTER 1

Where No One Has Gone Before

Humans are fascinated by space, unaware there's an entire universe waiting to be discovered within.

What if knowing who you are made your self-awareness so deep and so strong that your inner sage spoke louder than your inner critic?

Your true self is the part of you buried under an incredible amount of fear, limiting beliefs, painful emotions, and difficult past experiences. They make it hard for the real you to shine and create that fulfilling life you yearn for deep in your heart.

When you start unraveling what's in the way, an adventure of self-discovery begins. You begin to feel lighter, and your world becomes clearer. You see new possibilities. Slowly, you reconnect with your essence, and the roots of self-confidence grow deeper as you let go of what is not serving you anymore.

The first step to a-bun-dance for your finances is to decide to explore what's within. Beliefs and fears about money are countless, and you are invited to identify them so they can stop affecting your life in a negative way.

Diving inside Yourself

A lot about this world is pure fascination. All human beings have unique DNA. Even identical twins are different. Everything around and above us is one of a kind. Snowflakes never come twice in the same shape. Stars in the sky differ from one another, and so on.

All (or most) things are anything but the same. It is strange that for indigos, the profound, uncomfortable, and awkward feeling of not belonging in a world makes no sense because we are different feels like carrying the weight of the entire universe on our shoulders.

We yearn to be somewhere else, in another time and space, a different dimension, or another planet, but the discomfort seems to diminish a bit when looking at parcels of light in the infinite, dark sky on a clear night.

The belief that you don't belong in this world of duality couldn't be further from the truth, and it is an unnecessary burden on your heart. There is a purpose for you being here, and one way to find it is to take a journey of self-discovery.

Memories of a place where wholeness is the natural state of being are encrypted in you. Indigo children and adults have a particular energy, with a specific mission to accomplish.

Every system in place, whether it be education, politics, social standards, or finance, is obsolete. There is nothing more ridiculous and crazy than a bank making money on your account. Take, for example, the interest rate on credit cards. You throw money away—cash you could use to pay or do something else with—every time you pay interest to a financial institution.

That's one of the reasons you ought to develop an interest in managing money. No one else can do it for you. Learn mechanics. Know the numbers. If it doesn't seem legitimate, find out where it comes from, search for, or ask someone to help you find solutions, and you will feel more empowered.

By taking responsibility for your finances, you can reach greater independence and meet your needs in a way that allows you to create financial security and experience more abundance. Identifying your values, needs, and passions is also a key component.

Lesson Number 1: The universe provides when money is managed wisely.

I learned that lesson from a book, and at first, it can seem like the most logical thing. I can't quite remember where I was on my journey, but I know for sure it was an important milestone, a huge aha moment. The thought at the moment was so vivid that I still remember what it was: *If I just found out about it, a lot of people with ADHD probably don't know, and if they struggle with money, maybe I can share and teach what I've learned.* The idea for this book was born.

How could it be otherwise? If I am unable to manage $1,000, the same unhealthy habit will repeat with $100,000 or $1,000,000.

Becoming a wizard at overseeing what you already have means meeting the universe halfway. That alone is an excellent motivation to keep growing interest, don't you think?

You may feel confused right now, but living with a brain wired differently also means that the higher your interest level is in something, the more significant your intention. If something is boring, motivation, enthusiasm, and perseverance are anywhere but near. Boredom can also lead to impulsivity, and impulsive purchases can be a way to break out of what got you bored in the first place. Pay attention to see if it happens to you.

If something gets in the way, you must identify what it is. Otherwise, the same pattern keeps reoccurring. It's like a trap you can't get out of. Finding what might prevent you from moving forward in responsibly managing your finances is beneficial. This knowledge will come in handy when a distraction comes up or when you feel stuck.

Shifting your attention to what has already been accomplished is a great way out of a rut. Staying positive is too.

Lack of interest in finances and money management could explain why the portrait of the situation you find yourself in is blurry. If you've tried to oversee it before without much success, know that an ignition can't occur without spark. If nothing arouses your curiosity, you won't find it useful to get interested, especially with something you dislike, such as the tasks that go along with finances.

The goal here is to make investing your time worth it. Ignition of any kind needs to happen to get you to work, and it needs to mean something.

You may have the best tools, advice, or strategies to help you develop your money-managing skills. If you don't grow your interest, chances are everything will remain the same. Or you might experience change, but it will be temporary. We want long-lasting change!

Lesson Number 2: Interest ignition = making managing money matter.

If you have no clue what in this world can get you excited about finances—other than desiring more money—let's try to figure it out.

Becoming more and more conscious on many levels helped me become aware of how I behaved around money. Shortly after realizing the traditional workplace wasn't for me because I was aspiring to live a more fulfilling life that also gave me freedom, I ended up quitting my job as a journalist.

My time was dedicated to my business. Working hard and putting out so much effort for small or few results, I became more attentive to what my thoughts, beliefs, feelings, and behavior about money were. I still make sure to be aware of what they are, because they manifest in many different ways as I evolve. The awareness I gained was massive because of the limiting belief systems I learned as a child. Being a sensitive and intuitive child without knowing it at the time, I could sense that my mother's lack of money was disempowering. Even though she worked hard, she rarely had money to spare on things that were not a necessity.

When I wanted her to buy me something a little more expensive, she would say that she would buy it for me but not now because she didn't have the money. I could see the pattern playing out again.

Something was off. Looking back, I realized that working full-time with an excellent annual salary or from home; things were the same. I spent money in a careless, irresponsible way, which left me with little of it in my bank account.

Awareness is an essential key to change. You can't transform a negative behavior or habit without being conscious of its presence and how it impacts your life and the people around you.

When it comes to money, planning is a great skill to possess; so is having a sense of time and being able to project yourself for the future.

It's a real bummer that, in a lot of cases, the part of the brain that regulates the planning and projection into the future often underperforms in people with attention challenges. Both executive functions don't perform very well in this atypical brain of mine.

Having a deficit of interest can complicate your daily life, but not everything revolves around that.

I have come to believe that lack of planning skills is something I am challenged to learn. If you can easily function when things aren't planned, chances are you are extremely flexible, and that is a great asset. But planning is a necessity.

You must look beyond ADHD and identify your parents' and grandparents' beliefs, perceptions, and feelings about money.

Family antecedents are significant, and I don't mean, according to genetics, in what you believe.

If you are convinced that you will never be financially free because no one in your family was, that alone can sabotage your efforts and aspirations.

A **shallow belief** is a conviction of how you see or perceive an aspect of your life, yourself, or the world, something you think is true and belongs to you. It is something you adhered to because of what your parents or society taught you and from the education you received. It can also come from an intense experience of the past that either you or someone close to you went through. These beliefs influence your thoughts, actions, behaviors, and perception significantly.

A common belief conveyed by society is that you must work hard to earn a living.

Lesson Number 3: Shallow beliefs are filters that alter reality in an extremely disempowering way.

Vows of poverty made in a previous life can also affect your present life when it comes to money.

Identifying Beliefs around Money

Remember: limiting belief systems form in childhood and have a major impact in your life until you uncover and deconstruct them to replace it with the belief that serves your highest good.

Take a few minutes to center yourself by breathing deeply and slowly. When you start feeling calm, allow yourself to go back to childhood.

(Key)

Use the questions below as prompts to help you jog your memory about what the financial context was like when you were growing up.

What did you hear your parents, grandparents, and other close relatives say about money?

_____
_____
_____
_____

How did they feel about money?

_____
_____
_____
_____

How did they see money, and what was their perception of it?
___
___
___
___

What do you think about money?
___
___
___
___

How do you speak of it?
___
___
___
___

What are your fears around money?
___
___
___
___

How do you feel about money?
___
___
___
___

Do you know how both your parents reacted to the announcement of your mother's pregnancy with you regarding money? (Try finding out this information if it is unknown to you as it could reveal other beliefs).

_____
_____
_____
_____

Did your parents fear not being able to make ends meet?

_____
_____
_____
_____

Were they experiencing financial difficulties?

_____
_____
_____
_____

Were their parents (your grandparents) worried your parents would encounter financial difficulties?

_____
_____
_____
_____

Did money make your parents anxious or insecure?

_____
_____

_____
_____

What are the common beliefs that you and your parents share?
_____
_____
_____

Now that you have started to uncover parts of your belief system, how true do you think they are? Rate them on a scale of 1 to 10 (with one being totally true and ten far from the truth).

1 2 3 4 5 6 7 8 9 10

Keep in mind that other beliefs will come to the surface as you continue reading, and that's normal. It merely means they have a deeper root or that releasing other ideas opened the door for those to come out. The reason they show up is they don't serve you anymore.

Your Life Assessment

(Key)

The life wheel or circle is a tool to identify your level of satisfaction in various areas of your life and to give a visual image of what can be fixed.

This exercise is meant to provide an image of the areas—from finances to how often you use your creative power—that need more attention (the ones with lower scores) and those where you just need to keep up the good work (the ones with higher scores).

You can find several versions of this tool, which also helps in finding or maintaining balance.

I have renamed this exercise the ring of life as a ring symbolizes being united or a state of harmony. It also represents engagement, which is what you are doing as you evolve through this book.

All areas of life influence one another. The ring of life brings clarity and acts as a compass to point you in the right direction.

Completing the ring

- **Review all categories** - think about what a satisfying life might look like for you in each area. Be spontaneous and make a few copies or capture a picture of the ring for step 4!

- **Circle a number** representing your level of satisfaction. You can use colour or darken the sections with a pencil.

- **Mark the page** or make a copy of your ring so you have a reminder of the areas that need your focus and attention for improvement.

- **Repeat every three months.** Doing this exercice every 90 days will provide a visual of how things have evolved.

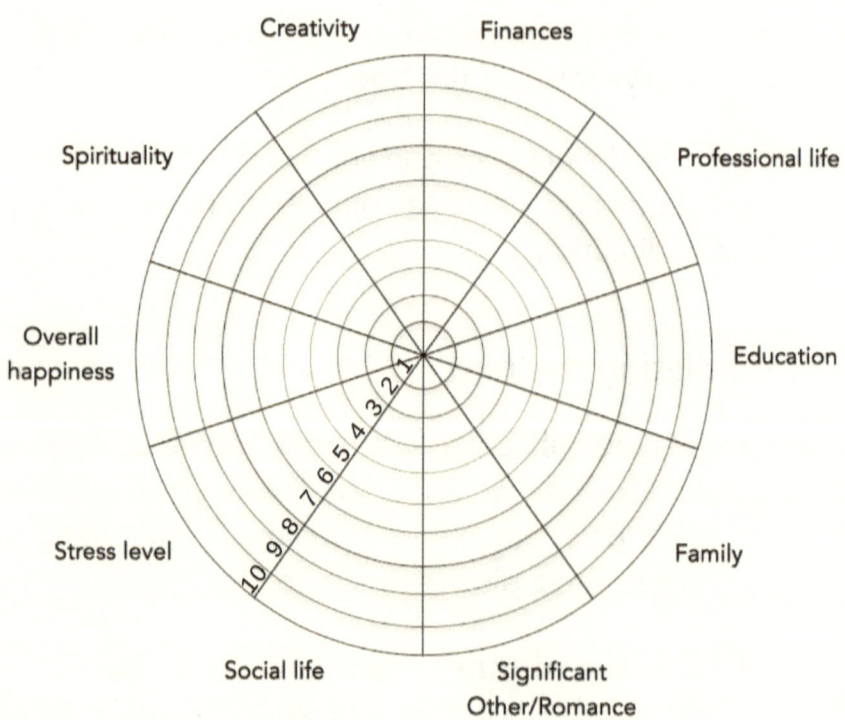

Adventure for Self-Discovery

Online resources allowed me to better understand who I am by identifying strengths, values, and talents, to name a few.

Your personality and learning styles play a huge role in how you think and do things.

(Key)

Discovering the characteristics that help define who you are will enable you to focus on the positive rather than the negative aspects. Here, I share some of my favorites.

What's Your Learning Style?

http://acktivv.com/en ($)

This test was first introduced in my ADHD coach training, and the results were quite an aha moment for me. There was no doubt that I was a visual learner and not so much an auditory one.

To my surprise, this test revealed other processing styles I was unaware of, allowing me to understand the way I learn, depending on what I am learning.

What Are the Specific Traits of Your Personality?

www.16personalities.com (Free)

When things are fun, my interest level rises high, and that's what the 16 Personalities test did. It groups four different personalities under four categories:

- analysts
- diplomats
- sentinels
- explorers

Each personality is defined under five aspects that outline the personality type:

- mind
- energy
- nature
- tactics
- identity

Both tests take about fifteen minutes to complete, and should you be curious, here's an excerpt of my personality type, which is bang on:

> The Campaigner personality is a true free spirit. They are often the life of the party. Still, unlike types in the Explorer Role group, Campaigners are less interested

in the sheer excitement and pleasure of the moment than in enjoying the social and emotional connections they make with others. Charming, independent, energetic, and compassionate, the 7% of the population that they comprise can certainly be felt in any crowd.

Friendly Reminders for A-Bun-Dance 4 Your Finance

1. The universe provides when money is managed wisely.

2. Interest ignition = making managing money matter.

3. Shallow beliefs are filters, and they alter reality in an extremely disempowering way.

4. You are not your beliefs, and you can change them anytime.

5. Self-discovery will help you find purpose.

6. Awareness is an important key to change.

7. Indigo children and adults have a particular kind of energy with a specific mission to accomplish so taking responsibility for your finances helps tap into deeper levels of healthy abundance (on all levels) so you can have more resources to accomplish that mission.

8. Complete the ring of life every three months to visually see what has evolved.

Lesson Recap

Lesson Number 1: The universe provides when money is managed wisely.

Lesson Number 2: Interest ignition = making managing money matter.

Lesson Number 3: Shallow beliefs are filters that alter reality in an extremely disempowering way.

Igniting the spark

- Find fun ways to grow your interest in money. Make it a game you enjoy playing. Allowing as little as 5 to 10 minutes every day to play with numbers will create a shift. Be aware of your energy flow and do it when your focus and concentration are optimal. Set a timer. Reward yourself.

- Pick 1-2 things in the ADHD questionnaire that could be improved and ask yourself: How will my life be enhanced if _____ (ex, paying bills late) is no longer an issue? Journal your answers.

- Now that you've identified one thing you want to change from the ADHD list, choose three doable action steps, you can take to move closer to achieving the improvement you desire. Set a deadline to keep yourself focused and moving forward daily.

- Play by keeping a record of your actions for the goal you chose in the previous step, note how you felt, and remember to do A-Bun-Dance to celebrate every victory, no matter how big or small. How can you make the celebration fun, so it becomes something that keeps you motivated?

CHAPTER 2

Only You Can Choose to Create a New Life

> If you're going to make a change,
> you're going to have to operate
> from a new belief that says life
> happens not to me, but for me
> or Life is nothing but a mirror
> of your consistent thoughts.
> -Tony Robbins

What if your life could be as amazing as you dream or envision it? Imagine for a minute that it is, and everything in that vision has manifested into a reality.

You have found inner peace. You are fulfilled, and you are living a meaningful life. Your heart overflows with love, joy, and happiness.

Nothing can disturb the inner calm as your foundation of self-confidence and self-love is unshakable.

Close your eyes and, without forcing anything or letting your ego interfere in telling you that what you are seeing is impossible, visualize this life you have created, using all your senses.

Take a few minutes, and then continue reading. You can also take a moment to write down what the visualization brought up. Know that it's okay if you encountered some difficulties envisioning your future self. The more you practice fast-forwarding into the future, the easier it becomes to do.

There are countless possibilities available to you. This chapter gives you the steps to set healthy boundaries for yourself and others and to identify unmet needs.

The world you've been evolving in may appear chaotic, unfulfilling, and dissatisfying. If the work you do is more like an obligation than a joyful venture, you may feel disconnected or trapped. You go through the motions, but deep down, you know something is off.

Any of this sound familiar? You've pushed your desires and aspirations deep down, the furthest you could, so you can keep going. Dreams you once cherished have slowly dissipated, becoming vague souvenirs.

Once upon a time, you could hear your heart's whisper and your intuition's guidance. Now, they've become voiceless, and your ego is louder, portrayed by the following:

- the nagging voice in your head
- the inner critic watering the seeds of self-doubt and brokenness
- the storyteller trying to convince you that you're not enough or unworthy

Over the years, self-care (genuinely knowing what you want, need, think, and feel) has faded away. Maybe you sense your life has been overtaken by people who suck up your energy, pollute your mind with their negativity, or bring you down in their spiral instead of lifting you.

You once were living in the light, but you are more often living in the shadow now. Clarity has turned into confusion. Confidence has transformed into a lack of it. Though you knew which direction to go at once, you are now circling around and around.

What I've just mirrored is a close description of how I felt at some point or another. The discomfort became so intense that, as mentioned before, I ended up quitting my job after exhausting my body and mind, leaving me drained energetically and emotionally.

After deciding that my health would never again be the price to pay for not listening to the signals and messages my body sent me, introspection became a new habit. The goal I was yearning for was finding purpose and meaning, even if I didn't know how to at the time.

When you become inner centered, meaning you stop searching for others' approval or answers outside yourself, you begin learning how to identify what serves your purpose and what tarnishes your true self. The best way I can describe it is that once the eyes start looking inside, a whole new world appears. It has always been inside you, waiting for you to discover it.

Whether it is renewing with strength, talent, or passion put to sleep for a while, values, or powerful, uplifting beliefs kept deep down under the surface, the treasure hunt is an incredible experience where you ultimately get closer to inner peace.

Lesson Number 4: Everything happens for a reason.

Over the course of life, there are many experiences, encounters, and situations passing through our journey without knowing the real lessons each one brings.

We must come to a state of full consciousness and awareness of these life situations and events. If we choose to ignore or deny them, they eventually repeat themselves over and over until we have learned the crucial lesson designed for our unique selves. That's a known fact for many, but not everyone.

Life provides experiences that allow the acquisition of new knowledge, room for growth, improvement as human beings, and complete wisdom. This is what happens when we allow ourselves to be open-minded and open-hearted. The challenges we face are there to teach us something, always.

The downside to that is falling into the victim trap, where you feel sorry for yourself, convinced that you are under a spell of some sort. This is far from how life works. If you have gone through recurring events or situations, you passed by a valuable life lesson that will only bring similar situations until you finally get it.

These repetitions, where you find yourself in the same position as in a vicious circle, are only a request for you to pay attention to something important in your life.

It can be that boundaries need to be put in place, or they are being overstepped. Maybe you need to learn how to say no or walk away from a toxic relationship. Perhaps you have lost yourself somehow; you feel stuck and are looking for ways to get moving forward again. Or it could be that your values and needs must be clearly defined and met.

Personal boundaries refer to space created around you acting as a protection of your integrity. They are a reminder that you need to take care of yourself and are essential for building healthy relationships. Establishing boundaries means defining who is allowed to enter your physical, emotional, energetic, and mental space.

If you have little or no awareness of the feelings and emotions you are experiencing or are unable to express and speak about your discomfort, you face a boundary issue.

Healthy boundaries are present when you:

- refuse to let someone be disrespectful or abusive toward you,
- differentiate a problem that belongs to you and to someone else, and you don't take others' issues on your shoulders,
- have respect for yourself and feel that real friends show more respect toward you,
- perceive conflict as a learning opportunity and find a way to resolve the problem so that everyone benefits from it,
- know that getting your needs met is your responsibility,

- have no feeling of guilt, anger, resentment, or fear about saying yes or no,
- feel stable and secure about your identity, and
- are confident, free, peaceful, and joyful.

Boundaries are a serious thing, and rigid ones are no better than lack thereof. When your boundaries are inflexible, it gets difficult to identify what you want, need, or feel. Struggling with loneliness or having low self-esteem can indicate that something needs to be reviewed. It can also manifest as distrust, fear of getting hurt or of someone taking advantage of your kindness, generosity and willingness to help.

Weak or nonexistent boundaries—or being a doormat—may be a sign of collapsed boundaries. How do you know if that's the case?

- You tend to tolerate disrespectful or abusive treatment.
- You fear being rejected or abandoned, so you say yes to almost everything.
- You ignore your feelings and take on others'.
- You can't figure out who you are or what you feel, need, think, or want.
- Needy and disrespectful people surround you.
- You can't be far enough when conflict occurs; you avoid it at all costs.
- You are a people pleaser.

Lesson Number 5: Setting healthy boundaries involves self-care and learning what you like, need, or want, and what you don't like, need, or want.

This applies to all areas of life, including money, and it's worth investing your time to identify what you like, need, or want and what you don't like, need, or want so you can make better choices when it comes to your finances.

Decision-making looks a bit like a roller coaster when it comes to money. Not all of them were thoughtless, but quite a few were—until the day I realized the pattern was spiraling my finances into a direction that no longer served me.

Unfortunately, years went by—I mean more than a quarter-century—before I finally paid attention to my relationship and behavior with and around money.

As I look back, I can recall two events that occurred a couple of decades ago that illustrate what I call repetition and lack of boundaries, which led to irrational decision-making and carelessness around money.

I had followed the wise advice I had received and invested $5,000–$6,000 in mutual funds, money saved up to pay for my college tuition. It was money I couldn't access easily. At that time, money was not an issue. I was working full-time, earning quite an amazing salary in the tourism industry. Life was good. Financial abundance was flowing. I had created a balance between saving and spending. Things were being done wisely. Or so I thought.

At the time, someone I was romantically involved with was in a difficult financial situation, and my burning desire to help, combined with foolishness and excess generosity, led to withdrawing *all* the money I had saved for my education.

Yep!

I kid you not!

What the heck was I thinking?

I honestly don't know.

How can someone be that stupid, crazy, and irresponsible?

I'd say well-intentioned but a little blinded by love.

How could I be so naive?

Excellent question. I haven't found all the answers and am not sure I must find them. What I needed to know or learn came when I wasn't searching, when I least expected it, or when I was ready to acquire the knowledge it had to provide.

Here's what I failed to take into consideration:

1. Thinking of or taking the time to evaluate the possible repercussions

2. Listening to my mother, who strongly disagreed and advised me not to withdraw my savings

3. Taking for granted that I was making a lot of money at the time

4. Setting an agreement for reimbursement and putting back the money in the account it was withdrawn from

5. Having healthy boundaries around money

Would things have been different had I known ADHD was part of my life, and it was partly responsible for sabotaging my wise planning for my education?

I honestly don't know. What I do know now, however, is that impulsivity definitely played a role in deciding to withdraw all the cash I had saved to be a good Samaritan.

The ironic part is that you'd think I'd learned the lesson after that, but. I did not.

So, fasten your seat belt because there is a second episode. It is insane because it involves dragging my mother into it.

Shortly after choosing to go on with my life, I ended up in a situation that felt strikingly similar. My learning experience was rewarding and beneficial for my growth. Desperately trying to fill the void of my absent father, I found myself emotionally dependent and searching for love for all the wrong reasons in all the wrong places.

Completely and unconsciously lost in someone else's dream, picturing success, fame, and wealth (I kid you not), I managed to convince my mother too.

Why she agreed to this crazy idea remains a mystery. She always worked so hard for what she had. On the other hand, my relationship with money was greatly influenced by hers and the beliefs she carried.

Anyhow, the plan was to buy the equipment needed for a project, and we were also planning to start our own company. To make a long story short, I convinced my mother to refinance the mortgage on her house to lend us $15,000.

What did this repetition teach me?

A whole lot. But the most valuable lesson is how unaware I was of my own value and how my values around money were blurry and my boundaries weak, making it easy for others to easily step over them.

It was also these events that made me realize how if we want others to respect us, we need to respect ourselves first.

I certainly was naive, but thanks to understanding what and why it happened, I became more cautious and alert.

You see, that is life happening for you. There's no point in blaming, cursing, judging, and getting angry at the people involved in the situations you find yourself in, or banging your head on the wall.

Living means learning. Some lessons are more expensive than others. In the long run, what really matters is what you do with the knowledge you acquire.

Why am I telling these stories that could be perceived as shameful and expose me to harsh critic and judgment?

Because this book is about helping you so you can break the cycles, change your behavior, grow your interest, and develop a freaking awesome relationship with money without walking the long and tumultuous road I've traveled on.

There were great insights, and for that, I am grateful. Now I know that knowledge doesn't have to be learned in an expensive way.

Insight Number 1: Being irrational, careless, and acting recklessly with money resulted in throwing away more than $20,000 in five years.

Insight Number 2: There is a direct link between how we treat money and how we treat and value ourselves.

Insight Number 3: Never skip steps 1 to 5 from the first story.

Insight Number 4: Having someone you trust, who has your best interest at heart and who you can rely on, is always good because he or she can be your voice of reason, especially when yours is silent. It's someone who will help you see whatever you don't and consider all possible consequences.

Lesson Number 6: Being wrong about something or making a mistake reveals an opportunity to learn what you need to move forward.

Before 2009, there was rarely a time in my life when financial insecurity manifested itself. After getting out of journalism school and realizing there were few openings in that field, I went back to working as a waitress in a restaurant, which paid very well.

When I moved back from Western Canada to Quebec, I was finally able, three years after graduation, to find a job as a radio announcer and a camerawoman at the local radio and television station.

My earnings were much less than what I was used to, but I was doing what I loved and acquiring experience. Life was great.

In early 2000, a private communication company hired me. My life and finances became even greater.

By saying yes to that job offer, my annual salary doubled. I remember hanging up the phone and exclaiming, "What am I going to do with all that money!" It was around $30,000 a year.

I might have been earning twice as much, but that increase didn't reflect one bit in my bank account.

Even though you think you have money under control, remember that you don't have it under control if you feel insecure about having money or if your managing skills are inappropriate.

Exploring and Defining Needs

What is a need, and how do you identify it? The Maslow hierarchy of needs, a motivational theory in psychological needs developed in 1943 by Abraham Maslow, defines five levels of human needs.

Maslow's theory established that people are motivated to achieve particular needs and that some take precedence over others. The most basic need is for physical survival, and this will be the first thing that motivates our behavior.

Once the basic need level is fulfilled, we'll be motivated to meet the needs at the next level up, and then the level after that.

One must satisfy lower-level deficit needs before progressing on to meet higher levels, such as growth needs. When a deficit need has been satisfied, it will go away, and our activities become directed toward meeting the next set of needs that we have yet to satisfy. These then become our salient needs.

However, needs that refer to growth continue to be felt and may even become stronger once they have been engaged. Once that type of need has been reasonably satisfied, one may be able to reach the highest level called self-actualization.

Levels one and two refer to basic needs. The third and fourth ones are associated with psychological ones, and the tip of the pyramid—level five—is all about self-fulfillment. At the bottom of the pyramid are physiological needs (level one):

- food
- water

- shelter
- oxygen
- clothing[1]
- sleep
- reproduction

Next are your safety needs—feeling secure in your job, property, resources, health, family, and social stability.

The third level is the need for love and belongingness:

- give and receive love
- appreciation
- friendship
- intimate relationship
- sense of connection

At the fourth level is the need for esteem: achievement, respect from others, self-confidence, the need to be a unique individual. The top and last level of the pyramid refers to needs for self-actualization, achieving one's potential:

- creativity
- spontaneity
- problem-solving
- lack of prejudice
- playfulness

---

[1] https://en.wikipedia.org/wiki/Maslow%27s_hierarchy_of_needs.

- authenticity
- self-sufficiency
- realizing inner potential
- experiencing meaning and purpose
- morality

What about Personal Needs?

Having needs is part of being human and is not optional. Even though personal needs resemble the ones in the Maslow pyramid, they are slightly different.

Personal needs come from something we didn't get as a child, a painful experience that left us scared and hurt. These needs can take over our lives negatively if we don't see to it that they are met.

Our soul also comes with deep wounds like abandonment, rejection, humiliation, abuse, betrayal, and injustice, with specific needs that also need to be met, and it is among the things I explore with my clients in holistic kinesiology.

A need must be met, and it can be fully satisfied by no one but us. The goal is to discover how we can fulfill our needs so that they don't impact us in a negative way.

If, as a child, you've felt abandoned or rejected, you've come to believe all sorts of things as the truth. In your child's mind, the pain had you draw conclusions that tainted your behavior, the way you see the world.

Internal discomfort will manifest in our adult life, but it originates in our inner child's need to be reassured, taken care of, and loved.

This data or so-called facts, feelings, and emotions were recorded in our subconscious without us remembering a thing about them.

Always keep in mind that an emotional reaction is one from the inner child. Take a moment and have a conversation with the little girl or little boy inside, and their voice will tell you what you can do to ease and heal the pain.

Here are a few beliefs I became aware of and adhered to after my parents' separation. Even though I was only three and a half years old, the feeling of rejection and abandonment left me deeply wounded with a lot of unresolved thoughts and feelings.

- I did something wrong.
- My dad didn't love me enough.
- I was unworthy of his affection and presence.
- I didn't deserve to have a dad.

- I wasn't important enough for him.
- I wasn't worth fighting for.

It also brought questions that never found answers in my child's mind (and heart):

- Where did my dad go?
- When is he coming back?
- Where is that feeling of being safe in his arms?
- Why hasn't my dad come back yet?
- When is this feeling of emptiness going away?

As I write these questions and beliefs, the pain of my inner child has greatly diminished. The little girl who grew up with a huge void in her life and became emotionally dependent, ending up in unhealthy relationships, has undergone deep healing of her wounded heart.

The woman wanting desperately to find in her romantic relationship the love she thought she had never received from her father, searching for worthiness and deservingness, wanting to be appreciated, accepted, and important, has learned to love herself.

Part of the work was to address those needs—find a process so these personal needs could be met. It took a while, but the outcome was worth it.

Lesson Number 7: We are responsible for identifying our unmet needs and finding ways to satisfy them.

It might come in handy to make the distinction between need, compulsion, obsession, and addiction. As has been mentioned, a need is something we carry, and if unfulfilled, it can dominate our lives in a negative matter.

A compulsion is something that fills us temporarily. It might also ignite an irresistible desire to act and has often gotten bigger than its usual form.

An obsession is something we can't stop thinking about, can't let go. We are preoccupied with the incapacity of meeting a need and can't focus on anything because we fixate on meeting that need. To a certain extent, we can also feel anxious about not having that need met.

An addiction is something that has spun out of control. There is also dissatisfaction with the outcome. This is frequent with gambling, where the gambler is not satisfied with the amount of money he or she has won.

Life flows with much ease when it revolves around your strengths, passions, and values rather than unmet needs, which take a lot of time and energy.

Unlocking Your Unmet Needs

 As you take a moment to let the information about needs and boundaries sink in, begin exploring your personal needs.

Which ones aren't met?

_____
_____
_____
_____

What actions or steps could you take to begin satisfying them?

_____
_____
_____
_____

How do unmet needs not serve you anymore?

_____
_____
_____
_____

What value would you gain in getting these needs satisfied?

_____
_____
_____
_____

How about Maslow's hierarchy of needs?
_____
_____
_____
_____

Is each level solid, or is there a weak one that could weaken the others'?

Setting Personal and Financial Boundaries

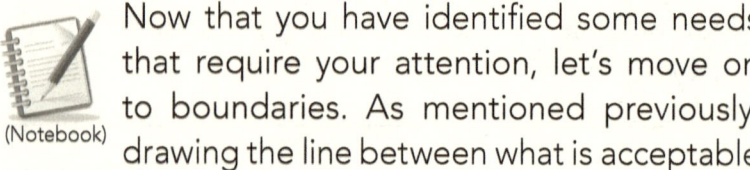
(Notebook)

Now that you have identified some needs that require your attention, let's move on to boundaries. As mentioned previously, drawing the line between what is acceptable and what is not in your life is an easy way to build confidence and assertiveness, increase your energy level, and so much more. When you have boundaries, and someone crosses the limit, they know it will come with consequences.

You want boundaries to be stable yet a bit flexible. Remember that rigid boundaries are as inefficient as not having any.

Not everyone will be pleased with you establishing your boundaries, but heck, right there, you may have identified someone who was violating that physical, emotional, energetic, or mental space so precious for you.

For boundaries to be efficient, your needs (the ones from the Maslow pyramid) must be clearly identified. First, go back to see what they are and write down those you wish to improve or desire more of in your life. You can use the 1 to 10 scale to facilitate your evaluation.

_____
_____
_____
_____

Friendly Reminders for A-Bun-Dance 4 Your Finance

1. Everything happens for a reason.

2. Setting healthy boundaries is about learning what you like, need, want, accept, or tolerate, and what you don't like, need, want, accept, or tolerate.

3. Being wrong about something or making a mistake reveals an opportunity to learn what you need to in order to move forward.

4. You are responsible for identifying unmet needs and satisfying them.

5. There is a direct link between how you treat money and how you value yourself.

6. Respect the boundaries you put in place to prevent others from overstepping them.

7. Life happens for you through different experiences filled with opportunities to grow.

8. Having money under control means you feel secure and are managing it appropriately.

Lesson Recap

Lesson Number 4: Everything happens for a reason.

Lesson Number 5: Setting healthy boundaries involves self-care and learning what you like, need, or want, and what you don't like, need, or want.

Lesson Number 6: Being wrong about something or making a mistake reveals an opportunity to learn what you need to move forward.

Lesson Number 7: We are responsible for identifying our unmet needs and finding ways to satisfy them.

Igniting the Spark

- Train your mindset every day. Choosing to create a new life means making different choices when faced with the same old circumstances. What new choices will you make each day to move closer to the improvement goal you set in Chapter 1? What old habits and limiting beliefs will you need to dismantle to make this happen? An entire universe awaits to help you, and there is no limit on how high you can soar!

- Raise your awareness. Your body speaks to you in various ways, and it will send signals when something gets out of balance or out of alignment with your values and needs. Connect with nature, go on a meditative walk to calm your mind. Doing a body scan — close your eyes and bring your attention slowly down to your toes and back to your head — to feel any change in your energy when presented with a financial decision, then take a few minutes to journal what comes up.

- Prioritize self-care. Make those me-time moments simple, light, and fun is a beautiful way to nurture yourself by doing things you love.

- Create a strong vision about what you want to manifest and include these three categories: financial security, financial independence, and financial freedom. Write, draw, collage what you envision for yourself, and spend 3 to 5 minutes reading it or looking at it every morning.

CHAPTER 3

When Integrity and Finances Collide

*The cave you fear to enter
holds the treasure you seek.
-Joseph Campbell*

Fears are illusions. They are not tangible, meaning you can't look at an object and say, "This is fear of lack." Although they feel real, they are a creation of the brain. Unfortunately, we react to our fears as if there were a real danger when, really, there's none.

There are quite a few of them around money, and my hunch is that a number of them are a heritage of our lineage (and the baggage we carry from past lives too).

But what is money, really, and why do we often feel out of integrity with it?

Erroneous beliefs about money are countless, and the idea is to help you identify as many as possible so you can:

- become conscious they are there,
- know how they affect your relationship with money,
- deconstruct them, and
- create new ones based on your core values and move forward.

Let's face it. Even though the system may not be working anymore, money has been around for quite some time as something we use to buy and pay for what we need as we exchange our time for a certain amount of it. For many people, I included, money is energy.

When I think about money, I picture everything good and beautiful it can help me accomplish in the world.

It helps to stay away from the negative, low-vibration emotions that have been associated with money: hate, jealousy, animosity, envy, cupidity, resentment, anger, and dishonesty. Some people are bitter or envy those who have more of it. Others wish it had never existed.

Money categorizes us in a social hierarchy with a strong belief that the rich get richer and the poor get poorer. In all this nonsense, false associations have been made.

One of them is the use of money to define what we're worth. Here's another one: having more of it makes us better in any way. And another one: wanting more makes us greedy.

These are some of the countless elements that have jeopardized our being in integrity when it comes to financial issues. Surely you can find a few more to add to the list.

When we are doing something and are not in integrity, nothing seems to be working. Difficulties arise. Challenges seem insurmountable. Struggles never end. It is the same with money. If our intentions and actions aren't in integrity, we are under the impression of falling short, that something is not quite right.

Being in integrity means we are whole, in tune with, or aligned with who we are, our best self. Having integrity, on the other hand, refers to morality and honesty. If this is one of your core values, it's easy to fall into the trap and get upset when you see injustice occur. You may feel like there is nothing you can do when so much can be done.

First, you can start by allowing yourself to start perceiving money as something intriguing and fascinating. It is a system you ought to be fearless about. Learn to use gentle words when speaking of it. Your thoughts are also very important. The more positive they are, the better.

You can then become motivated to understand why you have avoided looking after your finances all this time when the best person to take care of them is you.

Why?

Because should you decide to entrust the responsibility to someone else—be it a loyal friend, family member, or a professional—you will remain in control because you have learned how it works instead of giving your personal power to another individual.

The idea here is for you to acquire the basic knowledge rather than becoming a finance wizard. Being aware means giving value to your budget, knowing how much money comes in, and knowing what's left once everything is paid for. Being aware is also, as mentioned above, keeping a positive state of mind about money.

I would be lying if I told you that it's easy to get out of the negative rut, the fear of lack, and deconstruct shallow beliefs about money. Some unconscious programming is encrypted deeply. I've come to the conclusion that overcoming the huge challenges money brings into my life, and personal growth can only lead to an awesomely great and bright outcome.

There was a time when I looked at my bank statements, anxious and in tears because I was so much in debt.

Worries about not knowing how I would keep myself from drowning and fear of lack had taken over.

Lesson Number 8: Financial insecurity is a vicious circle that feeds your fear of lack, which attracts more of it and leaves you craving money.

Addressing my insecurities about money was a necessary step, and I began healing everything there was to heal about it. In becoming aware of my thoughts, feelings, and attitude toward money, I was able to let go of anything that wasn't serving me anymore— beliefs such as the following:

- I am not worth it.
- Being financially independent means that I need to be generating all that comes in.
- Earning money is hard and takes a lot of effort.
- I need to work hard to deserve it.
- There isn't enough for everyone.
- Only the rich get richer.
- The world would be a better place if money didn't exist.

When Integrity and Finances Collide

Every time a shallow belief comes up, I stop to question it. Who said such a thing was true? How true is it? Do I still need to believe this? Is this belief serving me? And if it's not, how can I replace it with an empowering one?

Feel free to try this exercise whenever you catch a belief trying to sabotage what you're doing, thinking, or feeling.

Another milestone in this journey is making sure I grow in my faith every day. Meditation, prayer, and introspection are some of the things I do at least once a day. They help deepen the healing process. Prayer and faith have brought an incredible sense of relief, and the more I feel at peace, the easier it is to be in balance.

Even in times when I had no idea how I would pay my mortgage, I trusted that all would be fine, and the money I needed would come in. And it did—every time.

The third habit I immensely benefit from is opening my heart to love and self-love. As this feeling grows stronger, it becomes safe to open your heart to the point where it's not even a bit scary to leave it wide open. No fear of being hurt, disappointed or betrayed. Opening your heart to love means first and foremost loving yourself, valuing, and embracing who you are, without judgment or criticism.

Lesson Number 9: The more you open your heart, the more love you will find within, and you can confidently diffuse it where needed.

As I continue putting my finances in order, a new relationship with money continuously evolves, which contributes to growing my interest. I now see money as a blessing for everything it provides, and I believe that there is plenty for everyone.

Opening yourself to gratitude is key.

(Notebook) What negative thoughts do you cultivate about money?
_____
_____
_____
_____

What can you do to release them?
_____
_____
_____
_____

How can you transform them to give them a positive spin?
_____
_____
_____
_____

What first step or action can help you open your heart?

_____
_____
_____
_____

Next, let's try to figure out your core values and personal standards. After needs, boundaries, and integrity, these will help you get a clearer definition of who you are.

Everyone has values and standards, but if you have no idea what your top five or ten are, it's nearly impossible to see the link between a value being neglected, ignored, or forgotten and the discomfort you may be experiencing.

Values reflect what is important to you; what makes your life meaningful and fulfilling. They help identify what inspires you and drives you, what you enjoy and would like more of. As you get to know and understand yourself better, your core values will change and deepen, so it's an assessment you can do every three to five years.

I first did the value exercise a few years prior to writing this book. Of the 145 values on the list, more than sixty of them spoke to me the first time around. I brought it down to about forty, grouped those who had a similar theme, and identified fifteen values.

Here are my top ten: authenticity, inspiration, abundance, freedom, creativity, integrity, love, passion, playfulness, simplicity. Since then, the other values that really resonated with me—but were less powerful at the time than they are today—including adventure, education, enlightenment, fulfillment, growth, and leadership.

As I got to know myself better in the last few years, and as life has provided me with the experiences and situations I needed to discover what my soul came here to accomplish, I try to make sure I refer to my values as often as possible.

When you remain engaged with yourself and your personal development, it is crazy amazing how, when you take the time to pause and look back, you see how you've grown, changed, and evolved, and that is the biggest fortune anyone can have.

Aspiring to a life of abundance, be it financial, love, friendship, compassion, beauty, creativity, or anything that sets your heart on fire, is accessible to everyone.

Walking into and accepting the darkness inside is necessary. Finding and facing whatever needs to be healed is also important to finally seeing our light shining.

Darkness can take many forms: fears, unhealed wounds, shallow beliefs, negative emotions and thoughts, lack of self-confidence, and deservingness. Interpret those as red flags indicating the direction of change.

Whoever or whatever led you to believe you weren't enough or were missing something was wrong. Trust me. I have carried this belief for a long time and probably over numerous life experiences.

You have more power than you think. Yes, you need to be willing to peel off the layers to get to your true self, the amazing human being created to live with meaning, whatever it is.

This may be new information to you, maybe not, but if you are *Indigo*, you are part of what is referred to as lightworkers. You are here for specific reasons meant to make a difference in the world to help transform it. Knowing who you are will help you uncover what those reasons are. Identifying your values is a great tool to do that. It will also bring you closer to your authentic self.

Values Assessment:

1. *Identify your core values* by putting a checkmark beside any value that resonates with you from the list below. Try not to be overwhelmed by its length, and do this step quickly without overthinking it. Feel free to add any value that is not on the list.

2. *Circle the values that are most important* from all the words you select in step one.

3. *Regroup any values* that fall under the same theme or category. Here's an example: guide, motivate, influence, impact, enlighten, teach, inspire.

4. *Choose one word within each category.* These are the personal or core values that are important to you. If you're up to it, utilize the space below, the one with the diamond, to write your definition or meaning for each one. You can also jot down what you do to foster it.

_____

_____

1. Abundance
2. Accountable
3. Accuracy
4. Alignment
5. Altruism
6. Autonomy
7. Authenticity
8. Balance
9. Belonging
10. Clarity
11. Commitment
12. Consistency
13. Contribution
14. Courage
15. Creativity
16. Credibility
17. Curiosity
18. Determination
19. Ease
20. Empowerment
21. Enlightenment
22. Enthusiasm
23. Fairness
24. Faith

25. Family
26. Flexibility
27. Freedom
28. Fun
29. Generosity
30. Gentleness
31. Growth
32. Honesty
33. Honor
34. Humility
35. Humor
36. Impact
37. Independence
38. Innovation
39. Integrity
40. Intuition
41. Kindness
42. Knowledge
43. Leadership
44. Learning
45. Love
46. Loyalty
47. Openness
48. Optimism
49. Originality
50. Passion
51. Peace
52. Playfulness
53. Prestige
54. Relationships
55. Respect
56. Self-love
57. Truthfulness
58. Unity
59. Visionary
60. Wisdom

Another Resource to Help You in Assessing Your Values

There are a lot of values tests on the internet. The Personal Values Assessment created by the Barrett Values Centre is a fun and interesting one to take (see link below). You are invited to select your values from a shorter list like the one above, and it will provide a report that includes a couple of exercises for self-development.

This short description from my report describes quite accurately who I am.

> From the values, you selected (compassion, creativity, financial stability, health, humor/fun, integrity, making a difference, personal growth, wealth, well-being (physical/ emotional/ mental/ spiritual) the following is clear:
>
> - You are a person for whom meaning is important. You have a strong set of moral standards, which are important in how you treat others and how you wish to be treated.
> - You are a person who wants to feel secure in the world. If these needs are threatened or not met, you will experience anxiety about not feeling safe or not having enough.

Your values show:

- a gift for thinking imaginatively and using your skills to produce new ideas help you to make a positive change in the lives of others,
- maintaining holistic balance is important to you, with efforts to keep in as good a condition as possible,
- you are in control of your finances and are well provided for is important to you,
- a strong sense of caring and feel empathy for others,

- a fun-loving approach to life and enjoyment for sharing good times,
- a faithfulness to yourself and your principles and the attempt to live your life accordingly, and
- a desire for opportunities to constantly develop and learn from your experiences.

The type of values you selected indicates that your individual capabilities are most important to you. From your choice of values, you also demonstrate care for the greater good (making a difference).

You can take the Personal Values Assessment at https://www.valuescentre.com/our-products/products-individuals/personal-values-assessment-pva.

Lesson Number 10: Start believing life is easy, and it will be.

Let's get clear on something right now. Lesson 10 doesn't mean you don't encounter any difficulties, nor does it imply that when things happen, your wishful thinking will make them all better. *To start believing life is, and it will be easy*, means that everything you come up against doesn't need to be a never-ending battle.

It boils down to these important things: attitude, perception, choice, love, and faith. Your choice of words is extremely important.

A-BUN-DANCE 4 YOUR FINANCE

Take a moment to reflect on the chapter you just read.

What's stopping you from creating the life you aspire to?

Where do you find strength when facing challenges?

Think of how you felt before starting this chapter.

What's different, or what changed?

Was there an aha moment?

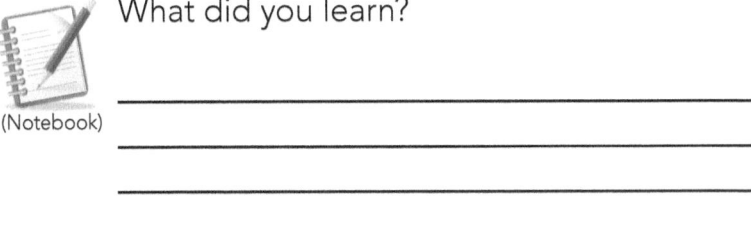
(Notebook)

What did you learn?

_____
_____
_____
_____

Friendly Reminders for A-Bun-Dance 4 Your Finance

1. Being in integrity means being whole, in tuned, or aligned with who you are, your best self.

2. Allow yourself to perceive money as something intriguing and fascinating.

3. Being wrong about something or making a mistake reveals an opportunity to learn what you need to move forward.

4. Cultivate a positive state of mind about money.

5. Financial insecurity is a vicious circle that feeds your fear of lack, which attracts more of it and leaves you craving.

6. The more you open your heart, the more love you will find within and confidently diffuse it where needed.

7. Make your core values the centerpiece of your choices and decisions.

8. Abundance, be it financial, love, friendship, compassion, beauty, creativity, or anything that sets your heart on fire, is accessible to everyone.

Lesson Recap

Lesson Number 8: Financial insecurity is a vicious cycle that feeds your fear of lack, which attracts more of it and leaves you craving money.

Lesson Number 9: The more you open your heart, the more love you will find within, and you can confidently diffuse it where needed.

Lesson Number 10: Start believing life is easy, and it will be.

Igniting the Spark

- Always ground yourself before doing your experimenting with numbers and money. Set an intention for the task. Close your eyes, breathe in slowly through your nose. You can even hold your breath for a few seconds if you want and exhale slowly. Repeat 5 to 10 times.

- Use your top core values as filters for decision-making. When you first run your options through your core values, you strengthen your mindset. Take the time to check-in with your body to see how it feels, so you become more aware. Create vivid images of what you want to manifest: use all your senses to nourish the feeling as if you already have what you want. When you believe you have all it takes to manifest your vision, it builds your faith muscle and reinforces your connection with yourself and the universe.

- Aim for consistency, not perfection. There is no need to worry about not getting right the first time. Focus on the game you are playing to spark and grow your interest in money.

- Pay attention to how and where resistance shows up. It may show up as disinterest, procrastination, or physical aches, just to name a few. Resistance is an excellent indicator that doing what you are doing will align you or keep you aligned.

CHAPTER 4

Acknowledge the Situation, and Embrace Change

When the winds of change blow, some people build walls, and others build windmills.
-Chinese proverb

When change comes your way, do you resist it or accept it and get excited, trying to find ways to make the most of it?

More often than not, resistance will come knocking at the door first. The winds of change blow us outside our comfort zone, the one where we are in a known territory with a sense of control, routines, old habits, and familiar experiences.

Acknowledge the Situation, and Embrace Change

We resist and hold on to what doesn't serve us anymore. We are spectators in our lives when the idea is really to let go and take risks, moving forward to the zone where new learning awaits us so we can reach happiness.

Moving out of your comfort zone is an important step in doing a-bun-dance for your finances, and finding someone who has the strength of your weakness can help you do that.

A transformational journey—it could be money or anything else being reshaped into something truly congruent with who we are—isn't always a joyride. Each phase comes with challenges to overcome, and oftentimes our first reaction is to show resistance.

I believe two things can happen when you reach a turning point or find yourself at a crossroads. The unconscious mind will continue circling like a merry-go-round, or awareness will be the catalyst for things turning around. It takes courage, determination, will, and resilience, but most importantly. Acceptance is necessary to face any challenge head-on.

The very moment I consciously chose to face everything that was deposited in my financial situation—issues, behaviors, abundance, blocking beliefs, repetition of unhealthy patterns, disempowering mindsets, emotions, and feelings about money—it created a huge shift.

This formula can be applied to any area in life: personal, professional, social, health, and so on.

Isn't it true that when a different outcome is wanted, some things need to change in order to be done differently?

At the time, either I created a totally different story or sank right into bankruptcy. Since the second option collided with my integrity and many core values, I opted for the first one. The rebel in me, the one who never did anything like anyone else, wanted to walk on an unknown path to see what she would find.

My ultimate favorite quote that sums up beautifully why and how I do what I do is from Apple's 1997 add campaign, *Think different*. I heard it for the first time at the end of the movie *Jobs*, about a human being I profoundly admire:

> Here's to the crazy ones. The misfits. The rebels. The troublemakers. The round pegs in the square holes. The ones who see things differently. They're not fond of rules, and they have no respect for the status quo. You can quote them, disagree with them, glorify and vilify them. But the only thing you can't do is ignore them because they change things. They push the human

race forward. And while some may see them as crazy, we see genius. Because the people who are crazy enough to think they can change the world are the ones who do.

Every time I read this, something inside me becomes even more powerful than it already is. The desire and conviction grow, and I know that I can contribute to making this world a place free of pain and sorrow by touching people, one heart at a time.

You can only imagine my desire and determination to do everything necessary to ensure I will never have to work for anyone other than my clients. It was and still is my driving force, the fuel that has me working on my relationship with money and finances on a daily basis.

Find Someone with the Strength of Your Weakness

Everyone has a large spectrum of talents, aptitudes, and strengths—things they are extremely good at that come as second nature. They use their genius, and it flows.

One of my talents, being highly intuitive, is to recognize the value and genius in others when they can't see it.

Whatever you are talented in, always try to think of ways to use it so that it can serve your weaknesses.

The goal here is not to invest your time and energy in trying to transform a weakness into a strength.

The goal is to use your talents to implement new habits and strategies around something that creates a limitation.

Fortunately, one of my best friends had the part of genius I needed with money, and since I yearned for radical change, I asked for her help.

Even if it wasn't easy to show my vulnerability and reveal the chaotic financial situation I was in, the pain was unbearable, and I wanted long-lasting solutions.

More so, I wanted to acquire the knowledge I needed to grow my financial intelligence. She gladly said yes on one condition: I had to do just as she asked without procrastinating or arguing.

That's one of the reasons I suggest finding the person who has the strength of your weakness. It requires that they:

- know you well,
- share a relationship based on mutual and total trust,

- understand where you come from,
- won't judge or make you feel judged,
- have succeeded with money and have yours at heart,
- have healthy habits like knowing—really knowing—how to count and has a system in place to keep track of their money,
- will be patient in teaching you what they know, and
- inspire you.

Another important thing is that you admire their relationship with money. It will give you insights about how you want to grow your relationship with this sacred partner.

The day I began paying attention to what I had ignored for so long was crucial, and the learning was priceless.

Even if it was wrecking and exhausting my brain to do the homework I was assigned, leaving me with a huge headache, draining my energy because it took so much attention, I focused and concentrated on exactly what was asked of me.

That's what it's like to have no, zero, nada, niet (actually spelled Het in Russian) interest in something. Our energy tank empties rapidly, our willpower is close to nonexistent, and we end up frustrated, ready to give it all up because we feel like such a failure, incapable of yet again accomplishing something, which adds a few more scratches to our self-esteem.

Sounds familiar?

These feelings escalate to thoughts that score ten on the scale of negativity, like a tornado spinning out of control.

When that happens, I suggest you do the following:

- Pause.
- Breathe.
- Look within.

After reconnecting with yourself, center your attention on your heart.

What's there?

What do you need to refocus on?

How can you change your perception to create a more positive impact?

Oftentimes, we fall into the procrastination trap about something we don't like doing or that we lack interest in.

But when that lack is for our finances, it's important to find one thing that will spark our interest, because the collateral damage is countless.

Acknowledge the Situation, and Embrace Change

Avoidance and disengagement will never create a positive feeling or outcome.

So, once that close friend or family member with the strengths of your weaknesses for money and finances joins your journey, make sure they understand and are able to show compassion for the challenges you are up against with ADHD.

One thing that might facilitate comprehension is to share a few things that came up in some of the exercises you did. It could be as simple as sharing your ADHD Money Questionnaire.

Don't be afraid to ask questions or feel hesitant when you require explanations about something you may not quite understand; otherwise, it can get in the way of what needs to be done.

Inhibition, completion of a task, boredom, procrastination, and inability to focus or pay attention are a few challenges that will show up.

Begin with one thing and then move on to the next, and so on. Give yourself permission to experiment different things.

Plan, at first, ten to fifteen minutes. Take a break and come back to the other tasks on the list. Do another ten to fifteen minutes. Choose a time when your attention and focus are optimal and go from there.

Use curiosity and creativity to generate a feeling of lightness into something that can give the impression of being heavy.

Color is a great example. What has been working for me is to use at least five different colors for files, markers, pens, and Post-its that match: blue, green, yellow, orange, pink.

My interest in money, numbers, finances, credit of all forms, loans, and everything in between began to grow the moment I became curious.

After learning the basics and practicing new habits until they became almost automatic, understanding a few principles like how much money I could save instead of giving it away in interest rates to the bank, I then became curious to see how good I would become at taming the beast, actually noticing a different outcome.

If curiosity about learning how you can have more money is something that works for you, your imagination will help you find the numerous avenues that can take you there.

If, on the other hand, going about this challenge is not something that resonates with you, whoever is helping you could be the one who guides you in finding something that will spark curiosity and awaken your brainpower.

Acknowledge the Situation, and Embrace Change

Asking questions is a wonderful way to nourish your curiosity.

Be assured that when you invest in growing your interest in money, what you put in will gain in value.

Friendly Reminders for A-Bun-Dance 4 Your Finance

1. Change often brings resistance, and your level of awareness about it is the best antidote to facilitate the process of transformation.

2. Choosing to face your financial situation and all that comes with it will create a huge shift.

3. Finding someone with the strength of your weakness will help your interest grow.

4. Use your talents to implement new habits and strategies around something that creates a limitation.

5. When feelings generate a high score on the scale of negativity, pause. Breathe. Look within. Center back to your heart. Acknowledge what's there.

6. Identify what fuels procrastination, and list a few key elements that spark your interest to avoid falling back into your old patterns.

7. Beware of avoidance and disengagement because they will keep you from creating a positive outcome.

8. Be accountable to the person helping you grow your interest in your finances and manage your money responsibly.

Igniting the Spark

- Remember: you are playing a game. The goal is to have fun improving your skills with money and finances. Take a look at the actions you are noting since identifying the things you chose to change in Chapter 1.

- Step out of your comfort zone. Doing things you're not comfortable with means going beyond fear of the unknown, lack of confidence, and finding excuses by taking a risk so you can discover new possibilities.

   To make your chosen improvement:

   - Where will you need to step out of your comfort zone?
   - What support will you need to do this in a way that will prevent you from getting overwhelmed or scared?
   - Identify 1-3 things you can do to support you in stepping out of your comfort zone. Identify 1-3 ways to challenge yourself to step outside your comfort zone to make

the improvement you identified back in chapter 1.
- How will you use the support you need to achieve this?

- Now that you've stepped out of your comfort zone despite your fears, you know fear is a pretense meant to keep you stuck. When you acknowledge this, you move into the learning zone. In the learning zone, you explore your thoughts, actions, and reactions to moving beyond comfort.

  It's not easy, though, and there will be times you feel like turning back.

  What strength can you rely on to keep moving forward and exploring your learning zone?

- You have the potential for greatness within you. Be brave, and you will achieve things you didn't know you could do/discover abilities you didn't even know were there. Then do A-Bun-Dane to celebrate.

CHAPTER 5

Assess Your Relationship with Money

Economy does not lie in sparing money but in spending it wisely
-Thomas Henry Huxley

What do you *really* know about your money history? Yes, money history. The one hiding in your subconscious mind linked to your ancestors.

Their history has an impact on the way you feel, act, and behave around and with money. The good news is that you can free yourself from those unhealthy patterns and transform your relationship with money.

You also created your own story about money through historical lineage. Parts of it were conscious, and others were not.

Assess Your Relationship with Money

As your level of awareness goes up, things will shift. Assessing your relationship with money is another important step in the exploration process that needs to take place before real, lasting changes can be made.

By now, you are aware that underneath the behavior, there are feelings, erroneous beliefs, emotions, patterns, and limited programming that need to be brought into light.

You are growing conscious about money. It is an important step in raising your interest in your finances. What you may not know is how your relationship with money can be unhealthy or toxic.

Since you are intuitively sensitive, money may be draining your energy, sucking it up like a famished vampire without you being aware of it.

Have you ever been in a toxic relationship or friendship where every time the other person left, you felt exhausted? And the only things you were able to do was lie down and rest because your energy tank went from full to empty very quickly?

Well, your relationship with money can create the same feeling.

As you do the inventory of your relationship with money, you might feel like it's making things worse or putting you in a crappy, would-rather-be-anywhere-else state of being.

You might not know this, but it is actually a sign that you are on the right track, and the more you dig out the ugly, not so pretty, and the totally disgusting in your relationship with money, the better.

The processes of confronting your beliefs and regaining the truth of how you feel about money are uncomfortable, unpleasant, and potentially painful. On the upside, and as mentioned previously, accepting what you find is absolutely necessary and will help ease the experience.

Tapping into strong emotions and shadow beliefs is a really great and effective technique to help decrease their intensity.

Something will come up to the surface that you won't understand, and that's okay. The goal here isn't to overanalyze to make sense of everything.

Erroneous beliefs, feelings, patterns, emotions, and limited programming will show up and bring a clear understanding. Others will be aha moments––a state of awareness that helps you become more conscious. I had a few of those, and they are delightful.

Whether it's something beyond comprehension, crystal clear, and full of meaning or totally mind-blowing, remember this one thing: everything knocking at the door of your consciousness is showing up because you are ready to acknowledge and release it. The reason is it doesn't serve you anymore, so *let it go* with a blessing for what it allowed you to learn and fill the space it leaves with love.

The ultimate goal is to ignite a feeling of joy and excitement, to fall in love all over again with money.

As I write this book, those two feelings have begun to take over my heart, raising my energy and vibration. Even though the sensation is quite euphoric, my awareness needs to be sharper, more alert to the negative self-talk that still comes up. Everything I dig out allows me to go deeper and deeper, with new shadow beliefs to uncover.

We all carry—or carried—fear of lack. Whether it's for time, love, money, or anything we yearn for or try to hold on to or grasp in a desperate manner, we are trained to respond in duality, or resistance instead of love, trust, and faith. What we don't have, we want more of, and somehow we believe that the only way to get it is by doing more.

A lot of things changed during and after I burned myself out at work. Striving as a TV journalist at the time, and believing my career meant everything to me, I ignored every signal my body was sending and found excuses for the fatigue and lack of motivation.

Getting up every day to do a job I was no longer passionate about became harder.

I had finally hit a brick wall, and the distress became so high that my body took control and collapsed.

Three years went by before I felt like myself again, full of energy and with a few more lessons learned.

It is one of my deepest beliefs that we face the challenges we are able to overcome. What would be the point otherwise?

Overall, I've always been healthy. No illness or disease is challenging enough that I could call it the biggest fight of my life. Burnout is the closest I've experienced to fighting for my health. It was quite the battle *and* the beginning of a new era. I just didn't know it at the time.

Earning a $50,000 annual salary was pretty awesome for a woman in her early thirties, but I treated money like crap back then, as if it weren't worth anything, and I believed it was always going to be there. Such an attitude was setting me up for a nasty ending and increased my chances of finding myself on financial life support.

And that's exactly what happened. Fear of lack came hunting me back, stronger than ever, ready to hit with its best shot, leaving me knocked out.

Phantom beliefs and thoughts coming from the dark side of the force took over:

I don't have enough money.

How am I going to pay for the mortgage this month?

There's more going out than there is coming in.

Debt keeps increasing.

Mind you, I forgot to add that I had impulsively quit my job not long after going back after an eleven-month leave. This turmoil must have happened about three years after.

Back then, every time I looked at my bank account balance, I'd feel my chest tighten with a rush of anxiety, fearing not finding a way out. Panicking about a situation that got worse as days went by, I felt hopeless.

Creating financial security was the only solution. Ironically, I ignored it for quite some time. The situation got so out of hand that the only choice I had was to go back to work because there was no way I would file for bankruptcy.

Stubbornness can come in handy, but it can also be a bitch when it drives you to make irrational decisions. You'd think that the anxiety, panic, and crappy emotions and feelings would be the kick in the butt to get me looking for a job, right?

I wouldn't be telling you this if they did, because I tolerated it for an entire year, until my back was actually against the wall, and no other options were in front of me to pull myself out of the mess I had created.

I chose to pause my dream to become an entrepreneur and found a job so I could relieve the anxiety I felt every time I had a bill to pay or upon checking my bank account balance.

From that moment on, I decided to take action looking for work, a specific request made to the universe. The response was a two-year contract that brought me peace of mind.

Money is one of the biggest challenges I face, but it is only the tip of the iceberg really.

Ignoring I had ADHD until I was forty, I was also unaware that finances could be such a challenge for our unique brain, bringing it higher on the difficulty scale.

The fear of lacking money felt like a tsunami had struck inside of me, causing terrible damage so that it became the breaking point. I decided it was time to get my act together and raise my awareness.

I decided the best option for change was to improve my relationship with money to create a more positive and aligned outcome. Little did I know it would also be the beginning of a whole new relationship with myself.

(Notebook) What have you discovered so far about your relationship with money?

_____
_____
_____
_____

What changes are you ready and willing to make?

_____
_____
_____
_____

What unhealthy patterns do you want to let go of?

_____
_____
_____
_____

Friendly Reminders for A-Bun-Dance 4 Your Finance

1. Keep aware that underneath the behavior, there are feelings, erroneous beliefs, emotions, patterns, and limited programming that need to be brought into light.

2. Growing conscious about money means you know if your relationship with this form of energy is healthy or toxic.

3. The more you unravel the ugly, not so pretty, and the totally disgusting in your relationship with money, the better.

4. Accepting what you find is absolutely necessary and will help make whatever is in the process of changing so much easier.

5. Judging yourself or blaming someone else lowers your vibration, and that's the last thing you want or need.

6. Not understanding or finding the meaning of what's come up to the surface is okay. Be careful not to fall into the overanalyzing trap, trying to make sense of everything.

7. Falling in love all over again with money means igniting a feeling of joy and excitement about it.

8. Building financial security is the antidote to diminishing the negative impacts of fearing lack.

Igniting the Spark

- Permit yourself to process and proceed in ways that support your unique brain type, even if they're different from what everyone else does. This freedom to use your creativity as an anchor for the vision you created will help you reach financial security, move to financial independence, attain financial freedom, and make the improvements you identified in Chapter 1 stick.

- Stay alert during your day, so you know your thoughts and emotions about money as they come up. Shifting your thoughts and feelings about money from negative to positive raises your vibration and enhances your relationship with money.

- Target 3 ways to improve your relationship with money to achieve the improvement you identified in Chapter 1. Make it fun by daring yourself to step out of your comfort zone and try new things.

- What three things will you dare yourself to do to improve your relationship with money over the next 90 days?
- How will these things help you achieve your goal from Chapter 1?

CHAPTER 6

Know Where Your Cash Flows

*Beware of little expenses. A small
leak will sink a great ship.
-Benjamin Franklin*

Navigating an ocean of numbers may not be your thing, and the reason why doesn't really matter. Even if there is a link with ADHD, anyone facing the challenges that come with uninteresting tasks can find ways to face them head-on.

A leak in your finances can be small but cause considerable damage. Knowing what they are makes it easier to stop them or, better yet, prevent them. Here's an important key to your a-bun-dance: money flows in and out, and there is plenty to provide for all your needs.

Know Where Your Cash Flows

Money is energy, something to exchange, a way to acquire material objects and honor our responsibilities. It is also the most powerful tool to allow those who follow their mission of making a difference in the world to serve on a much larger scale than anyone can imagine.

Yes, we need it.

Yes, it needs to be moving, coming in and going out.

It is also an area where the list of erroneous beliefs expands.

In French, the word for money is *argent*. Simply translated, it means silver. Shiny and in some way precious, it has a very powerful vibration.

Have you ever noticed how shiny things, more often than not, get our attention?

Knowing where your money flows is an important component in your relationship with it, and with a visual reminder, a symbol or image more meaningful than a few numbers indicating your account balance, you transform something rather abstract into something more tangible.

Imagine this for a moment: regardless of the amount of money you have in the bank, visualize each dollar is a beautiful diamond, shining brightly under the sunlight. Now close your eyes and picture those precious jewels.

What's the first thing that crossed your mind when you saw the diamonds?

How would you describe the feeling in your body?

What emotions showed up?

How was the overall experience in this short visualization?

What beliefs came knocking?

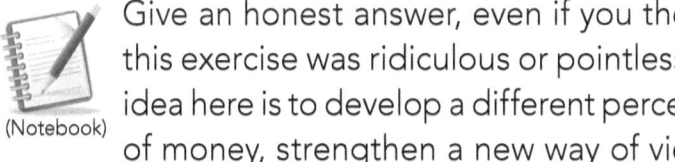
(Notebook) Give an honest answer, even if you thought this exercise was ridiculous or pointless. The idea here is to develop a different perception of money, strengthen a new way of viewing it, and discover what makes it fun.

_____
_____
_____
_____

The thing with ADHD is that what we don't see we forget or has little meaning for us.

Maybe a one-dollar bill (or coin, depending on your country's currency) speaks to you, and that's freakin' awesome, but for me, it was crucial I make it tangible.

Why? To become conscious of how much money comes in and how much goes out. To nourish that awareness and take responsibility for my finances in a time where debit and credit cards have made it super easy to lose track and lose control.

Trust me. I did both. More than once. However, the desire to tackle the issue and overcome the challenge was more powerful than the disinterest.

Discovering that having fun and making work feel like play was a core value that gave a huge spin on how I did things.

So, from having no interest whatsoever and not wanting to learn to gaining interest in numbers required trying a variety of strategies. I ended up having such a blast that I was inspired to share my most valuable, helpful tactics.

How is your cash flowing right now?

Are there any leaks? Meaning, are you losing money to the bank by paying interest on your credit card every month?

Have you ever thought of reviewing your spending habits?

How do you keep track of the money you spend?

If you don't, what system could you put in place or who could help you set one up?

Know Who Owes You Money

Our tendency to forget things makes it so easy to lose track of people who borrowed money from us and never paid it back. My motto for this is simple: I don't lend money to anyone, and if I do, it's on very rare occasions.

It's a nonnegotiable one because I know the chance I will forget is likely to score high on a scale of 1 to 10, and because ignoring the leaks through which I lose diamonds can be very costly.

Identifying money leaks and keeping a close eye on them is extremely important. Discipline is key, and I suggest you set time aside once a week/month to check and write down the amount of money that leaked, so that whatever needs to be adjusted can be before things get more out of control.

I like seeing these numbers, especially with credit cards, because in the end, the interest rate increases the amount you paid for whatever you bought, and the money you freely give to the bank could be used, for example, to make a payment on your bill.

It might also mean that you have to decide whether you continue using your credit card or leave it at home for a few months so you can focus on decreasing the burden by following these steps.

Creating a Weekly Money Ritual

Money ought to be considered a sacred partner, and there's more to be discovered about that in the last chapter of the book. Nourishing a healthy relationship with money so you can experience the feeling of a-bun-dance for your finances is crucial, and a ritual is … essential. Here's are the actions I put in place:

Step 1: Start by planning a thirty-minute appointment (to start) in your agenda once a week. This is as important as a doctor's appointment, so there's no skipping or forgetting it. Check all the transactions to make it easier to keep track.

Find the fine line on your credit card bill stating how long it will take to pay what you owe if you pay only the minimum amount each month. You might find extra motivation to move on to the next step.

Step 2: Have a book or a document on your computer to keep track of every amount you pay in interest (personal loan, credit cards, etc.). Using Excel will give you a clear monthly view as well as a cumulative amount of how much money leaks through each year.

Step 3: Find someone you will be accountable to, a body double (someone to do it with) or both, as it really helps fuel the motivation and the perseverance to accomplish steps one and two.

Our uniquely wired brain comes with a load of challenges that shouldn't be served as excuses. Understanding what and how your difficulties show up in your life is extremely important. Only you can take charge of ADHD and your finances.

It's been said many times, but I insist on this one: be sure to make the process fun. A special space can be created in your home where you do an a-bun-dance overview and get curious about the results. Make it a colorful, vibrant abundance project. Light a candle. Play your favorite music.

The ambiance I create changes depending on how I feel and what I need. Sometime, comfy clothes, meditation music, and my favorite crystals are a must.

Other times, I am so excited that I sit in front of my computer, and I get into my weekly ritual without any specific ingredient.

One thing I always try to do before beginning is taking a moment to ground myself with my favorite elixir blend.

Over time, this weekly appointment became more of a sacred moment—a chance to connect with money on a much deeper level, and it makes a huge difference.

It assures I do this coming from the heart. Whatever the scenario may be when you look at your diamonds—how much came in and how much went out, including the ones that allowed you to honor your financial responsibilities and those interest charges on loans and credit cards—always, always, always stay in your heart.

Be aware of the tasks you don't like to do so much and observe your thoughts, feelings, and beliefs. No need to rush during the process, because chances are you will find great insights. Allow for this introspection to take place. Then use these questions as prompts to see what you discover in the process.

What comes up?

What wounds are triggered?

What childhood events resurface?

Everything you will discover is a rough diamond ready to be transformed so that you can heal your relationship with money.

Practice makes perfect, and there will be times when you forget to do it or do not feel like doing it. Be gentle with yourself if it happens and make the intention to do better next time.

Justifying What You Need or What You Need Is Justified

Some things resonate more than others, and what is great about knowledge is how powerful it becomes when shared. How and why we spend money can reveal extremely valuable information.

We may at times justify a purchase, and that can be a sign it might not be something of necessity.

Treating ourselves to something special is totally okay. However, starting to pay attention to the inner dialogue going on when you buy something will indicate if the item is something you really need or if you are finding pretexts to purchase it.

Is it something you need right now? If so, why?

Nowadays, it is so easy to spend money—and trust me, I absolutely love buying things. What changed in the past few years is choosing what I buy with care and a few rules to follow. These are applied to any purchase, from small ones to bigger ones—groceries, clothing, makeup, books, and so on.

Next, I choose my words carefully so I don't feed fear of lack without realizing it. More often than not, I will say these things:

- I choose not to buy this right now.
- I choose to save money before buying this.
- I choose to be wise about this purchase and give myself a few days.
- I decide not to buy on impulse.

My goal is not only to purchase things I need but also to make sure it is something that is aligned with who I am and my values. I want to make sure it creates a feeling of being strategic with each purchase and fulfills a real need, not just one I created and justified.

Friendly Reminders for A-Bun-Dance 4 Your Finance

1. Knowing where your money flows is an important component in your relationship with it because it's hard to fix a leak when you don't know where it comes from.

2. Having a visual reminder (meaning real money, not a debit or credit card) is a great way to help become conscious of how much money comes in and how much goes out.

3. Keep track of who owes you money because with ADHD comes forgetting easily, and that can become a big money leak, especially if you have a generous heart and people taking advantage of it.

4. Plan a thirty-minutes appointment (to start) in your agenda once a week. This is as important as a doctor's appointment, so there's no skipping or forgetting it. Check all the transactions to make it easier to keep track.

5. Create a special space in your home where you do an a-bun-dance overview, and get curious about the results. Make it a colorful, vibrant abundance project. Light a candle. Play your favorite music.

6. Understanding what and how your difficulties show up in your life is extremely important. Only you can take charge of ADHD and your finances.

7. Whatever the scenario may be when you look at how much came in and how much went out, always, always, always stay in your heart.

8. Make sure you are in a state of deep gratitude when you pay your bills to ensure your thoughts, emotions, and mindset about money are keeping your vibration at its highest.

Igniting the Spark

- Keep your focus on the outcome you wish to create rather than the bumps on the road that make you feel stuck.

- Remember that changing your relationship/thoughts/feelings (whichever makes the most sense) to your finances is a process. Give yourself space to explore and keep it fun and light, so it remains enjoyable.

- Stay engaged in the financial processes in your life by assessing your level of interest during the day. This way, you can make adjustments when you lose interest so you can build better habits. The 1 to 10 scale can be a great tool.

CHAPTER 7

Finances, Self-Worth, and Nutrition

*Live from the inside out. Your mind,
body and spirit are interconnected.
Nourish your soul with mental
and physical wellness.*
-Janet Taylor Spence

The next step to a-bun-dance for your finances is to look at how you nourish yourself: body, mind, heart, soul, and spirit.

How you value yourself is also extremely important as it will affect your mood and drain your energy without you knowing it. Keep an open mind as you dive in and continue on the journey that began with reading this book.

Finances, Self-Worth, and Nutrition

Depending on the food, thoughts, and feelings you choose, there will be an impact on your overall well-being, because every part of you mentioned above is linked and affects the others.

Until we break the vicious pattern of trying so hard to fit in, playing the victim, and yearning for love and acceptance, we will continue having internal turmoil. And for what, really?

Another common thread I've noticed is that a lot of us are emotionally dependent. I sure as hell was, and not too long ago, I realized I had also fallen into the trap of being financially dependent on my spouse at a certain point.

Maybe emotionally dependent clients are the type I attract, because I've been there. Who knows? But it sure got my attention.

This craving for love and the attempt to fill the inner void with something coming from the outside may result in emotional eating, overspending, or any other form of addiction: coffee, cigarette, alcohol, drugs.

If you wonder where this is all going, bear with me. It may not make any sense, but stop for a moment and reflect.

Is your life in balance right now?

When you did the ring of life exercise, what areas needed more attention?

There is a connection between every area in life, just as your body, mind, soul, emotions, and energy are connected. What you eat affects your gut, thoughts, emotions, and energy positively or negatively.

Refined sugar, artificial sweeteners, food additives, pesticides, and other chemicals deteriorate the microbiome (intestinal flora), which works closely with the nervous system and the brain.

They also have an impact on certain ADHD symptoms like hyperactivity, impulsivity, inattentiveness, lack of focus, and self-focused behavior that will disrupt your mood and turn your emotions upside down.

Brain fog is also another downside of what you eat … or not. It inhibits the ability to think clearly and be sharp. Gluten has that effect on the brain.

Nutrient deficiency is the second element that will affect emotional balance, hyperactivity, impulsivity, change of behavior, and mood.

Eating clean and nutritious foods in addition to taking high-quality nutritional supplements free of food dyes, chemicals, and heavy metals assures that you won't add to the toxic load in your body.

Finances, Self-Worth, and Nutrition

While taking care of your physical vehicle, the same rule applies to emotions and thoughts. They will manifest, and you will feel them intensely.

Filtering thoughts and emotions is the next step. As you become the observer and practice filtering your thoughts, you might notice or uncover something deeper: shadow beliefs and fears that seem powerful.

Those negative thoughts and false beliefs can fit into different categories. Money is definitely one, and so are these: family, love, relationships, work, kids, and the way you perceive yourself.

Growing a garden of positive thoughts takes time because deconstructing negative thinking—or worse, rumination—doesn't happen overnight. Transformation requires time and effort as growing into your true self can't and won't happen overnight.

In the previous chapter, I mentioned how deciding to create an entirely new relationship with money also meant major transformation in my relationship with myself.

Well, what I know to be true is that your relationship with yourself is the only one that will last a lifetime, and the more you grow, the more it will deepen.

Even though I've become better at filtering my thoughts, there are times when they show up stronger than ever. I remember this one time when I was totally lacking confidence about bringing my big vision to life. All sorts of feelings and emotions stirred inside, but mostly it was sadness. A deep and profound sadness was bringing my spirit down, and unsatisfying thoughts came trampling over me.

The negative thoughts spun out of control, so what came about was the release of the emotional overload with tapping or EFT (Emotional Freedom Technique). While I was tapping, these crazy affirmations transpired.

Somehow, I had this overwhelming feeling of disappointment for myself and my spouse. I wasn't where I wanted to be in my life. And the only things getting in the way of this big vision of mine, better known as my dream come true, were doubts.

What threw me during this ongoing cycle of releasing and crying, releasing and crying, was that I thought I wasn't the woman my husband deserved. Holy shit. Where did I get that crazy idea? We've been together almost twenty years and share an amazing relationship.

From the moment I decided to create my own business, I could count on his morals, along with a tremendous amount of encouragement and, yes, financial support. Deep down, I feared being a burden on him by not being an equal partner financially.

Then guilt showed up. He was away for work for two weeks, and while I was at home, knocked out with a cold, he was earning money, and I wasn't.

After tapping into my senses for several minutes, I felt the emotional disturbance calm down and felt deep gratitude for having such an efficient technique to free myself from disempowering beliefs.

That morning, even if I had tried to challenge my thoughts and beliefs by asking the following questions, I don't think it would have worked so well:

Is that thought/belief true?

Who said I had to believe this thought?

How can I transform this negative thought/belief into its opposite?

Why? Because the root cause of the initial feelings and emotions was way deeper. It had to do with self-worth.

Later that morning, honey phoned me, and even though his call was unexpected, the timing was perfect. After sharing the beliefs I had, he said to me, "What made you think I am not proud of you? Of course I am."

When asked if he believed I would succeed in bringing my vision to life, he said, "Of course I believe you will succeed. Why wouldn't you?"

I went on with my day, writing this book, sharing my message with love and joy in my heart.

A garden of positive thoughts means that each of them is a seed that you plant.

Before becoming luscious and beautiful, the seeds need to be nurtured and nourished. Cultivating is a discipline that goes much deeper than thinking a positive thought.

You need to feel it very deeply and own it entirely. Let it submerge your heart, every fiber in your body, every bone, tissue, organ, and cell, until it becomes what you vibrate.

Acknowledge your worth along the way because that too impacts your relationship with money.

Self-Worth versus Self-Esteem

Living with a unique brain comes with being passionate. It fires up our creativity and imagination, having us go on and on like the Energizer Bunny!

The other cool thing is that when attention and focus are ignited by interest, what we're having difficulty with isn't an issue anymore. We reach the hyper focalization zone and end up losing track of time, even forgetting to eat unless our stomach sends us the signal it's time to feed ourselves.

When talking about the challenges we face daily, self-esteem is high up on the list, but how about self-worth? Is there a difference between the two, or are they the same?

Self-esteem and self-worth are two different things as the first one is how we feel about ourselves, and the other is how we value ourselves. Yes, there are similarities, and the line that defines them is thin, but it's there.

Self-esteem is often built on what other people think about us or say to us. God knows a lot of those opinions and remarks are too negative for us living with this differently wired brain.

The *being an outsider* feeling has a great effect on our self-esteem. Not fitting in, being highly intuitive or an empath, having a strong and intense energy, and thinking outside the box is who we are, and they are just a few of the many things I love about uniquely wired brains.

The spectrum of the challenges we face have been used as weapons against us, leaving the majority with the conviction that everything we try to accomplish is a battle we could compare to David against Goliath.

Simply put, self-esteem has a lot to do with what we do. It forces a comparison with others rather than paying intrinsic attention to our value.

That's what self-worth is based on: the value we attribute to ourselves. It's about who we are and what comes from within or lack thereof.

Through the journey of identifying what made my relationship with money so difficult, I came to realize that it was closely linked to my self-worth.

For some reason, we have the erroneous belief of not being enough, not deserving what we yearn for, and that is so not true.

Underestimating our value is extremely damaging and limiting because it places us in a disempowering position. It's like a fight you can never win, until you become conscious that the higher your self-worth is, the better.

It will positively influence every decision you make about money and financial abundance, especially if you are a soulpreneur, a healer, or lightworker.

How You Value Yourself Is How You Value Money

If you don't believe you are worthy, what do you think money will be worth to you?

If you don't recognize your value, how do you think it will affect your perception of money?

If you don't acknowledge your value, what impact can it have on your financial abundance?

If you are convinced that you need to be and do more to have more, how do you believe it will influence how money comes to you?

If you ignore what makes you worthy of being more, having more, and deserving more, where does it leave your financial situation?

I could go on, but I trust that you get the picture I am trying to paint here. The lower your self-worth is, the lower your vibration. What you vibrate will translate to what you receive from the universe. More importantly, if you are not open to accepting your worth and being willing to receive, you'll be feeding into your fear of lack and the belief that what you ask for will not be granted.

Increasing my level of self-worth is something I continue to work on, mainly when I am developing new services, products, and offers in my coaching practice. The reason for that is simple: it is imperative I always validate within to make sure it is aligned with my life's purpose and vision.

The same rule applies if I need to invest in myself to learn what is necessary to reach the next level of success and financial goals. To get there, I need to go through the next phase of personal transformation.

It's also about being aware of how what I create nourishes my self-worth. When we take a close and honest look at how we value ourselves as individuals, it can really shake our foundations.

We realize how hard we have been on ourselves and how harshly we've judged ourselves. We've raised the expectations so high that it left us falling short. Discovering and recognizing the amazing potential we have is what we ought to bring out of the shadows.

Becoming aware is about coming to the realization that something isn't right or aligned with what we want in life, and that's when we take charge to change it.

After finding what sparked my interest about money and finances, which was mainly finding meaning and understanding so that I knew what needed to be transformed, dismantling the fortress that blocked my ability and capacity to recognize, acknowledge, and believe in my self-worth was quite the task.

Finances, Self-Worth, and Nutrition

As I look back, being able to see where I was and where I am now, as hard, challenging, and confusing as it was to bring those walls down, the efforts, tears, uncomfortable situation, and roller coaster of emotions were worth it.

The comparison might sound funny to you, but increasing my self-worth felt as good as the day I chose to clean up my lifestyle habits, because I knew the better nutrients my body got, the more incredible I would feel physically, emotionally, and mentally. It would benefit my nervous system and improve concentration and attention, just like cutting off gluten lowered physical hyperactivity considerably.

Developing the Habit of Increasing Your Self-Worth

Increasing my self-worth means nourishing my thoughts with empowering ones and challenging my inner critic, or ego, to make sure my efforts are not contaminated or influenced by negativity. It's building an entirely new mindset, powerful and strong like titanium.

It is also a means of discovering any programming, either from my ancestors or past lives, to neutralize any repeating behaviors, limiting beliefs (because there will always be some), and anything that can jeopardize what has been accomplished to break free of my toxic relationship with money.

Identifying my soul's most important wound, the one she came into this life's experience to transcend, was another crucial element in the process. As mentioned before, body, mind, emotion, energy, and spirituality are all connected. The wounds carried by the soul have an impact on the other elements, which affects every aspect of our lives, since they are not separated from one another.

One episode in particular enabled the releasing of deep sorrow about money. Without being able to pinpoint what was wrong that day, I went for a walk. Nature always has a calming effect on me, and it's where I feel most connected to God, to my higher self.

I remember feeling as if the universe had forgotten about me because even though I had asked for my financial situation to improve, it felt like my requests were unheard. (Who do you think I was feeding? Fear of lack and feeling of unworthiness monster!)

As I was repeating a mantra with the word abundance, the word *abandon* came out instead.

Without even knowing it, I was carrying the belief that the universe had abandoned me. The pain was so deep. My arms opened wide in a receiving gesture, looking at the sky, repeating and crying in profound sorrow: "I deserve and am worthy of financial abundance" (or something like that!).

Assessing what was getting in the way—that day—was a tedious and demanding task because there was a lot of crap there, and facing our weaknesses, flaws, and darkest secrets is not easy. It takes courage, resilience, and a lot of self-love.

All the suffering imprisoned in the heart also needs to come out, and the only way to achieve that is to unlock the fortress around it. Is it painful? You bet it is, but it is also the most effective way to let out what's been separating you from developing and growing your self-worth. Get your heart to take the lead instead of your ego.

Guilt is a sign our ego is trying to run the show. I remember feeling guilty because my desire was to earn more and work less.

Did I believe it was possible? Yes. I still do. Even though that belief has grown stronger, it is a challenging one. It is put to the test on a daily basis by other negative beliefs and thoughts.

The thing is every level of growth confronts whatever is locked up inside and needs to be released so we can continue moving forward, one step at a time.

For me, it is about deserving and being worthy of building an empire without tremendous hassle and battles.

Of course, giving life to a big vision is challenging and will bring its load of long hours as well as hard work. It will ask of me that I face new phases of deep transformation, but I am confident that I am worthy of the life I dream of, that I am deserving of it and that the universe will cocreate this big vision with me as long as I am aligned with my life's mission.

If I'm not, it's up to me to do whatever is necessary to realign myself and experience the success of my positive impact and philanthropist contribution in the world, the financial freedom and all forms of abundance I deserve.

It is said that what you admire in other people, you already have within. Women such as Oprah, Pink, Marie Forleo, and so many more incredible leaders are on my list. Even though they are successful, what I admire the most in those women is how they use their talents and unique gifts to make a difference in people's lives.

That's the league I aim for as an indicator of the impact I want to have in the life of indigo adults like you.

The more I shine, the more I will be able to inspire you to shine.

The more I allow my light to be seen, the more I can help your light ignite in you.

The more I show that who I am is the only way to be, the more you will have that same profound conviction.

So how do you recognize, acknowledge, and celebrate your worth?

Do you deeply feel deserving or believe you are not?

Do you recognize your value for what it truly is, or do you minimize it?

Do you believe you need to work hard to deserve what you want?

Do your results seem as high as the efforts you put in?

Do you believe you need to do more to have more?

Do you sometimes feel like you haven't done enough or that there is something you didn't do and that's why you don't get the results you seek?

Do you believe that by giving more, you receive more?

Thinking you are not deserving, lacking recognition of your value or worth, believing you need to work harder than necessary, not getting the results for the efforts you put in, doing more to have more, feeling as if there is something you didn't do and thinking that's why it's not working are signs that a lot of thoughts, beliefs, and fears need releasing so you can invest more time in building and reinforcing your self-worth as well as your mindset.

Out of the many challenges I had to and will have to face with money, since every level of financial growth calls for a change of mindset, recognizing my value has been and will always be number one on the list. It always begins within.

The best example I can share to illustrate that is with my business. After acquiring the knowledge and competencies, I invested a lot to create Indigo Coaching—and in myself, not so much.

Balance is key in life, and the same applies to business. With each level of success you aim at come the challenges you need to overcome in order to get there.

When you create a business or anything born from passion, it really is the extension of who you are. Your kids are an extension of who you are. This book is an extension of who I am.

Finances, Self-Worth, and Nutrition

I was determined to reach the next financial growth level and knew I needed to work with a coach to help me in that important transition and transformation.

Even though I had done a lot to recognize my value, I remember almost fainting when she told me the investment required. There was a wall, and I crashed right into it. Without even knowing it, I believed I wasn't worth that kind of investment.

Fortunately, as I became more and more conscious of the belief system and the fears behind it, I began addressing them. Fear of not being enough was a strong one, and it is present in many of us.

Negative, limiting thoughts, beliefs, and emotions are part of life. Like your body needs food to function, how you nourish what you think, what you believe, and what you feel is a choice only you can make, and it comes down to always going back to loving yourself unconditionally.

(Notebook)

As you are in the final pages of reading this book, take a moment to pause and reflect on this new journey you have embarked upon. I encourage you to revisit all the pages marked by a Post-it, any exercise you neglected doing, and sections that awakened an unpleasant feeling to see if something has changed.

Think of how you felt before reading this chapter and how you feel now.

Is there a difference in how you feel about finances, self-worth, and nutrition?

_____
_____
_____
_____

What new awareness has arisen?

_____
_____
_____
_____

Were there any aha moments?

_____
_____
_____
_____

What's the most valuable thing you learned?

_____
_____
_____
_____

(Diamond) Now, celebrating is as important as pausing and reflecting. When we take the time to celebrate something, we anchor certain feelings and emotions: joy, contentment, completion, excitement, and gratitude, to name a few. The most crucial part in your celebration is boosting your self-esteem and allowing your awareness of these rewarding feelings to shine through.

So, what would you like to celebrate at this moment in time?

Friendly Reminders for A-Bun-Dance 4 Your Finance

1. Breaking the vicious pattern of trying so hard to fit in, playing the victim, and yearning for love and acceptance calms internal turmoil.

2. Refined sugar, artificial sweeteners, food additives, pesticides, and other chemicals deteriorate the microbiome (intestinal flora), which works closely with the nervous system and the brain.

3. Transformation requires patience as growing into your true self can't and won't happen overnight. Keep in mind to be gentle with yourself.

4. Cultivate a garden of positive thoughts by nurturing and nourishing the seeds. It's a discipline that goes much deeper than thinking a positive thought.

5. Self-esteem has a lot to do with what we do and forces a comparison with others rather than paying intrinsic attention to our values. Self-worth is based on the value we attribute to ourselves. It's about who we are and what comes from within or lack thereof.

6. Recognizing and honoring your value must always be number one on your list, especially when your inner critic is speaking louder than your inner sage.

7. Nourishing what you think, believe, and feel is a choice only you can make, and it comes down to loving yourself unconditionally.

8. Remember to pause and reflect on your journey. Be grateful for the acquired awareness and the growth experience.

Igniting the Spark

- How can you find ways daily to reinforce your value and worth? Find 1-3 actions you can practice to build a positive perception of yourself in these areas.

- Increasing your value will change how you value money. One way to increase your self-worth is by detaching yourself from what others think or believe about you. Seeking validation from others is an excellent indicator that you are giving it too much importance. Determine your reference to what defines your value. Embrace your unique brain type and its particular way of seeing the world.

What do you need to do to detach from the opinions and points of view of other people? How do you define your value, and what do you see in your life that reinforces your definition?

- Always remember, the Universe has infinite possibilities beyond what you can imagine. Don't just settle for what you think is "enough." Dream bigger!

CHAPTER 8

Be Account-*Able*

I want to try the impossible
to show it can be done.
-Terry Fox

What you believe you can't do or accomplish stays true until you decide that things are going to be different. Two of the greatest strengths that are very common with ADHD are determination and perseverance.

Yes, they also fall into the challenge category, but I've noticed that trying until we succeed, even if we get discouraged along the way, is rarely an option.

A characteristic of a strength is that it is practiced until it is mastered. This goes for becoming better at growing your interest about money even if you have ADHD.

The idea is to have a system in place that keeps you moving forward, and being accountable is one of them. So is knowing your financial archetypes. Yes, there are different avatars that are part of and influence your relationship with money.

Accountability is something most coaches use with their clients. It means that if you are accountable to someone for something, you are responsible for it and must be prepared to explain your actions, or nonaction, to that person.

Developing accountability is a way to give a deeper meaning to an important step toward growing interest in money, even if you have ADHD.

Oftentimes, what we don't understand doesn't make sense, and the goal here is to help you find something that will bring some comprehension and meaning.

For the longest time, I didn't give a damn about what went on with my bank accounts. I couldn't care less about what went in and what went out. If a check bounced, I didn't even care about the fees I was paying for absolutely nothing.

What's fifty dollars out of the window?

It's fifty diamonds that I could have used to buy necessities like groceries or to treat myself with something special.

It was two hours of work if I earned twenty-five dollars an hour.

It's a nice dinner at my favorite restaurant.

It's fifty dollars that I couldn't put toward an upcoming vacation.

It's devaluing my worth, and it's not being financially smart.

And why the heck would I want to grow my financial intelligence?

Because people who develop or have that kind of intelligence have more money, and I want to be in that category! When you appreciate money for all the amazing things it can contribute to, create, and accomplish, it will ultimately lead to a better and brighter life.

What also appears in the word accountable are the words account and able. To me, being account-*able* refers to the ability of managing your accounts with cleverness and discipline.

When you look at your financial situation, being account-able is huge.

Be Account-*Able*

One of the first steps in assessing your financial health is the money questionnaire at the beginning of the book.

Then you identified money leaks by looking at where your money was going. You identified fears and beliefs along the way, reflected on your relationship with money, and celebrated your efforts to break out of the cycle you are in.

Throughout the process, you learn the skills to become more responsible with money, meaning taking responsibility for how you interact and respond to it. You will instantly see a difference.

Becoming account-*able* means looking at your credit card statements and reading the part in very small print telling you how long it will take to finish paying the entire amount if you only make the minimum payment. That's if no purchases are put on the card.

Becoming account-able means learning how to read a credit card bill so you know the following from month to month:

- How much was charged on it?
- How much did you pay back?
- How much did you pay for insurance on your card (if you have protection)?
- How much interest did you pay?

Being account-*able* means being aware that you pay interest on interest, meaning that the percentage is calculated on the amount due.

Being account-*able* means keeping track of every single dollar and every cent that is given away and adding the task to your weekly and monthly abundance appointment. Over the course of a year, you will be surprised at the amount of cash flowing out when you add all the fees on your credit cards, your personal line of credit, and those for your bank account transactions.

(Key) I encourage you to go back and do the exercise for the past six months. Depending on the time of year you are reading this book, make it your duty to cumulate twelve months, as it will give you something to refer to.

Things resonate with me a lot more when they are visual, so your chart could look something like this:

Month	Credit Card 1 (19,99%)	Credit Card 2 (11,99%)	Line of Credit (5%)	Mortgage (6,85%)	Total Fees Paid
January					
February					
March					
April					
May					
June					

Be Account-*Able*

(Notebook) What would you rather do with that money?
_____
_____
_____
_____

How do you feel when looking at the column of total fees paid?
_____
_____
_____
_____

What emotions does it bring to the surface?
_____
_____
_____
_____

What strong limiting beliefs can you identify (find at least three)?
_____
_____
_____
_____

How about tapping into your senses on those beliefs?
_____
_____
_____
_____

Discovering Sacred Money Archetypes®

Another fascinating thing and major turning point that brought comprehension and meaning on my journey was when, after finally saying yes to working with that coach I mentioned previously (the one who told me what investment I was going to make in me, and I almost fainted), I discovered my Sacred Money Archetypes®.

Finding out what they were was a major game changer. It explained my relationship with money for the past twenty-five years and what I needed to learn to balance and honor the Sacred Money Contract of my main archetype, which is Maverick. Like the main character in *Top Gun*, this archetype likes taking risks and is not afraid of taking financial ones at all.

One of them, the Accumulator, actually had a lot to do with the writing of this book without me even knowing it. This archetype's personality is a bit like a banker, someone who keeps track of the money that comes in and goes out. It's the accountable (or account-*able*) one.

Knowing what needs to be paid when and how much is being account-*able*. So is paying bills on time.

Knowing what you spend your money on is being account-*able*. Learning how to use a credit card is too.

Be Account-*Able*

Keeping track of your expenses is being account-*able*.

Growing interest in your finances is being account-*able*.

Knowing a few tricks like escaping the fees that you can avoid by maintaining a certain amount in your bank account is being account-*able*.

My financial institution, for example, doesn't charge a $12.95 monthly fee if my account balance is over $3,000 or diamonds. Times twelve months, that's $155.40 of diamonds that stay in my pocket. Maybe you think that having that much money is useless because of the following:

- There are bills, a mortgage, a car, tuition for the kids, groceries, gas, insurance, and so many other things to pay.
- You want to get out of debt, break the cycle of survival mode, and never look back because it becomes draining.

I hear you when most of the time all we can think of is surviving any given period. Our perspective gets lost, and making plans for the future seems unreal and unrealistic.

Having a few thousand dollars in your bank account to save on monthly fees may not be a priority just now, but give it time. As you do the work, you will

A-BUN-DANCE 4 YOUR FINANCE

realize that all the extra fees could have been put to something you may have needed the money for, and I assure you everything will click.

The pathways of the false beliefs we've walked on are deep without us knowing it. Remember, at any time you can choose a new pathway, release what needs to be released so you can continue moving forward with beliefs that serve you and lift you up instead of bringing you down.

(Notebook)

When we are in survival mode, it is nearly impossible to have a long-term vision. This exercise is meant to help you change the scenario.

If it feels awkward or unnatural, don't worry, and remember that you are deconstructing something that's been part of you for a very long time.

Read the question. Close your eyes and let your imagination guide you (not your ego trying to tell you this is stupid or useless). Put every sense into allowing this experience in. Stay in it for a few minutes, open your eyes, and write down what came up—what and who you saw, how the scenery was. Repeat for each question.

Breathe in slowly through your nose. Breathe out slowly through your mouth. Imagine you are financially secure and abundantly supported. Breathe in again slowly through your nose. Breathe out slowly through

Be Account-*Able*

your mouth. You have money to spare and no debt at all. Breathe in slowly through your nose. Breathe out slowly through your mouth.

Remember that your imagination is guiding you …

What does a day in that life look like?
_____
_____
_____
_____

How and where do you feel your new life in your body?
_____
_____
_____
_____

Who did you transform into in this new life?
_____
_____
_____
_____

What action can you take to be one step closer to your new life?
_____
_____
_____
_____

What do you need to help you get there?

_____
_____
_____
_____

What do you wish to celebrate?

(Diamond)

_____
_____
_____
_____

Friendly Reminders for A-Bun-Dance 4 Your Finance

1. Appreciate money for all the amazing things it can contribute to, create, and accomplish.

2. Being account-*able* requires practice in knowing what goes on with your money: earnings, expenses, fees, interests, and so on.

3. Paying your bills on time is being account-*able*, and it also helps keep good credit.

4. Focusing on what you don't have increases fear of lack and keeps you in survival mode.

5. Being attuned to the vibration of gratitude sends a powerful message to the universe that you feel and are secure around money.

6. Abundance is a state of being, not something we aim for.

7. As your relationship with money becomes healthier, false beliefs will show up, and at any time, you can choose a new pathway.

8. Release, release, and release some more so you can continue moving forward with more self-worth, faith, and self-confidence.

Igniting the Spark

- Keep things fun by creating challenges for yourself. Continue moving out of your comfort zone by doing something new or that you've never done before and always wanted to try. Draw inspiration from what brought you joy when you were a kid. You could laugh for no reason, crank the music up, and dance in your living room. Do whatever brings you joy.

- Identify 1-3 action steps to put in place and practice that will increase your sense of security and help you achieve the improvement you identified in Chapter 1. Having a goal enables you to overcome your fear of lack/scarcity so you can move out of survival mode and tune into the frequency of abundance.

- Practice tapping (EFT) to free yourself from anything you wish to let go regularly.

CHAPTER 9

Money as a Sacred Partner

There is absolutely nothing wrong with wanting more money. The motivations behind that desire are what matter.

As your journey reading this book comes to an end, I really want you to take a moment to celebrate. You've made it this far, and that needs to be acknowledged.

The last step for creating a-bun-dance for your finances is to raise your level of awareness a notch and consider money with respect and honor its sacredness. It's also about building a reserve and learning to say no.

Money as a Sacred Partner

When you've had a bad or toxic relationship with money, some patterns are harder to break than others. It's really the same as being involved in a toxic sentimental relationship or friendship.

Going from a love-hate relationship to considering money as a sacred partner is a huge shift but not an impossible one.

We think that the hardest part is to get out of it, but it's really the healing that needs to take place that can be demanding. From my experience, whenever resistance shows up, the healing or the transformation is always harder.

Resistance has multiple faces, so how do you recognize them? By paying attention to what goes on in your body, the physical sensations and emotions as well as the inner critic inside your head.

I don't pretend to have all the answers, but resistance is a manifestation of our ego trying to take control to protect us, even in absence of danger. Many phases of transformation, including those with money, were an open door for resistance to show up for me.

It would manifest in the transition process as I was moving from an old way of being to a new one.

Resistance can be pictured as a trap to keep us exactly where we are, so the tough decision is this: do we continue playing the victim or rise above it to undergo a process of change, accept transformation, and reshape ourselves by owning up to the responsibility of our lives?

In any situation, our reaction and what we decide to do with it is what makes the difference between the old and the new.

I could believe that I should be working instead of dedicating my time to writing this book. Or I can believe that while I am in alignment with my life's purpose, using this unique gift of writing, the universe is working with me.

The second option is the one I choose because by doing so, it increases my faith that I am not alone in working on making my big vision come more and more to life.

Whatever thoughts and beliefs are going through your head right now, know that I understand where you are coming from because I've been where you are.

I blamed others instead of taking responsibility. I played the victim for God knows why. Did I know how to stop being a victim? Nope. Was I consciously a victim? Good question.

Sometimes you don't even realize that part of you has taken over. The defense mechanisms are so deeply programmed that it becomes second nature.

Our subconscious is so well trained in doing it that it's like being in prison without even knowing it, keeping us locked inside ourselves, and until we open up our heart to release the pain, hurt, and suffering, we're trapped.

Saying Yes and Saying No

Have you ever been proposed to do or gotten involved in something, and shortly after, you realize it wasn't such a good decision to say yes?

Learning to say no is part of being human, and it's not the wisdom we were taught at a young age. Having a unique brain, we've also experienced or have had to face a lot of criticism and negative comments. They created a belief system that led us to become people pleasers.

Saying yes or no to people is similar to saying yes or no to money—accepting or rejecting it, if you prefer. How can you be assured your choice is the right one?

Chances are you know this, but as we tend to forget the simplest things, the first thing to ask yourself is, "Am I doing this because it brings me joy or is it because I feel obligated?"

When my answer comes from a place of love, it adds power, and there is no more doubt I've made the right choice.

Like anything, it's a daily practice, and practice makes perfect.

If you want more money beyond it serving the purpose of being financially free, you will have to choose to accept it in your life. There is absolutely nothing wrong with wanting more money. It all depends on the motivations behind that desire.

The main reason I desire financial abundance is to make a huge impact in the world and leave a legacy behind so that what I create changes the lives of people throughout their journeys on earth.

To achieve that, the most valuable thing to me is to consider money as the sacred partner that will help make that vision come true.

No One Can Make You Believe You Aren't Enough

Unless you allow them to, there is not a human being in the world who can make you think that there is something you don't deserve. No one. Adhering to what someone else believes about you is handing over pieces of your inner power.

All of us have free will, which by definition is the ability to choose between different possible courses of action unimpeded. Even if someone thinks the worst of you without justification, their opinion belongs to them and should not be considered as your own.

Stay aligned with the following:

- who you are
- your authentic self
- your values

What you think and believe about yourself is all that matters, and as long as what you are doing and try to do comes from the goodness of your heart, nothing should weaken that.

Here too, there will certainly be hidden limiting beliefs and habits that you'll need to free yourself from, and you can refer to the questions in chapter 1 to help you identify them so they can be replaced with more empowering beliefs.

Remember that having strong boundaries, nourishing your self-worth, and self-love are excellent ways to protect you away from negative influencers.

You Have More Power than You Think

Always remember that. We are so much more powerful than we believe, which, in reality, is really what scares us. Marianne Williamson sums it up beautifully:

> Our greatest fear is not that we are inadequate. Our deepest fear is that we are powerful beyond measure. It is our light, not our darkness that most frightens us.

We are here to shine, sparkle, glow, be ourselves, and live our lives not according to what others and society expect from us but according to what our soul came here to accomplish.

As we go up the levels of consciousness and step in deeper and wider into our light, we need to undergo a profound transformation and major change in order to ignite the light within us. Once this occurs, we become less afraid of opening our hearts and have an understanding that keeping a wall up for protection and the constant fear of being hurt will not result in a solution.

Every day, I have conversations with God. They vary in topics and intensity. I remember two of them like it was yesterday. The first one took place a few years back when I was so fed up with carrying my ancestors' baggage handed down about money and everything else I knew wasn't my own to drag along.

There was a conviction in my words I could feel deep in my heart while saying, "If I have to come back for another life experience, there is no way in hell I am coming back with the baggage I came in this life with. No way. So provide me with whatever I need to release and free myself from as much shit I don't need, because I won't go through the same sorrows. If and when I come back, I want to begin where I left things and continue. Not start over."

This feeling hasn't left me since, and under no circumstances will I have a groundhog life in the next one!

Another conversation took place just before accepting to finish the project of writing this book. For the longest time, I abandoned and rejected the part of me that came with the amazing gift of writing. In the big vision I cherish, it occupies a major part.

Thing is I was scared even though I know it is through my books that the door to the inspiring life I am creating will open. Deep in my soul, I knew ignoring and rejecting that part of who I am came with consequences. Accepting and embracing it was vital in order to be aligned with my life's mission.

In desperation and blinded to the solutions available for me to get my business to expand to the next level of success and obtain my big vision, I said, "From where I stand right now, I'm pretty much asking for a miracle."

One year prior to that day, I had said no to acquiring a publishing package to give birth to this book, the main reason being money.

Back to my plea for something magical to happen. The same day, I received a call from the same publisher, informing me the package I shut the door on had become available again.

This time, my answer was yes. No lingering fears of not having the money, nor did my ego try to make a diversion from my biggest and wildest dreams.

(Key) How about the unique gifts you have and should be using but are not? Everyone is here to serve a purpose, and our unique genius is often how we do it. Take a moment to find this or those things that bring you in that zone of incredible talent, and find out why you stopped using that genius of yours.

What unique gift have you left in your childhood and why?

_____

_____

Money as a Sacred Partner

_____
_____

What erroneous beliefs made you forget about that special gift?

_____
_____
_____
_____

How can you reconnect with it?

_____
_____
_____
_____

What do you need to give life to your dream?

_____
_____
_____
_____

(Diamond) Now, what do you feel like celebrating? What have you uncovered or discovered, and what new awareness has it brought to light?

_____
_____
_____
_____

Why Is Building a Reserve Crucial?

It has already been mentioned that fun is one of my core values. I remember one exercise that definitely caught my attention in my coach training. You may have heard of the cash register exercise. Another version is the prosperity game, which consists of having an amount of money deposited in your bank account every day.

Day one, the Devine Bank deposits $1,000, $2,000 the next day, $3,000 the third day, and so on. This can be done for fifteen, thirty, sixty days, or more. You can double the amount deposited each day if you choose to play on a shorter time period. Every day, you take a few minutes to write down what you do with the money.

Here are a few of my statements:

- Day 1: Pay $1,000 on my Visa. My intention is to be financially full of abundance with lots of money to build my Altruist Empire (share) and have a lot to create time freedom (spare).
- Day 4: $3,500 on Visa number two that has now a zero balance. Give $200 to charity, catch up on paying overdue bills, and buy traveling insurance for my trip next month, $300.
- Day 5: $5,000 to the local women's shelter.

- Day 6: Give it all to charity: $4,000 to the local palliative nursing home for people with cancer and $2,000 to an organization that helps feed the less fortunate.
- Day 21: $5,000 into creating a foundation for ADHD (charity) so it can help people I serve have access to support for them or their kids, $5,000 for a traveling budget, and $11,000 into savings. Declutter my office desk and feel great beginning the week in a clutter-free environment.
- Day 27: Adding $15,000 to the house in Hawaii project, putting $5,000 into savings, and $1,000 to seven families who are praying for a money miracle this week.
- Day 34: Accepting the divine $34,000 deposit with humility and putting $14,000 for the house on the Big Island, $15,000 on the mortgage on our house in Montreal, and giving $5,000 to the True Health Foundation.
- Day 51: $51,000 into savings and enjoying it while waiting to be inspired for what I wish to do with it.

A reserve can be built for money, and that exercise is one way to begin envisioning what it would be like to actually have money saved up and plenty to share so you can contribute to making this world a better place.

Yes, it can seem utopic, unrealistic, and unachievable, but if it becomes a burning desire and you think you can do it, even if you don't know how, it may just become a reality.

(Notebook)

Building a reserve is also applicable to your energy. All work and no play will drain the life out of you and bring heaviness. That's why balance between every sphere of life is important, and you have the ring of life to help you create or maintain this balance (you can redo the ring every three months).

Time for yourself, expressing your creativity, acknowledging your genius and your value, and laughing on a regular basis can help you do that.

So, how can you build your reserve from now on, and how will you remember to use this on a regular basis?

_____
_____
_____
_____

Do you need prompts? And if so, what are they?

_____
_____
_____
_____

When will you start?

_____
_____
_____

Determining What the Next Step Will Be

(Gold bar) What you do with the knowledge you've acquired and how and when you decide to put it into practice (if you haven't already) is now up to you. The results can only come if you engage in growing your interest in your finances.

You might need to try different ways to go about it before you find a process that works best for you. It is extremely important that you are willing to adjust when challenges come up and above all refuse to quit when you feel like giving up.

Always be present and aware of how ADHD traits and difficulties show up. Pause if you need to have a better understanding of what's going on *before* you get discouraged.

Most importantly, remember to celebrate!

What will be your plan of action?

_____
_____

_____
_____

What outcome do you wish to create in growing interest in your finances?
_____
_____
_____
_____

What could get in the way of attaining that goal?
_____
_____
_____
_____

How will you be accountable and become accountable?
_____
_____
_____
_____

Allow Yourself to Receive

When you allow yourself to receive more and more, and you believe results will eventually manifest and trust that they are coming, shifts will happen. The ups and downs of life won't undertake the efforts you have put in a project you are passionate about.

It will create shifts and open new doors leading to new possibilities.

Find inspiring stories to read, such as books that will increase your genius and reinforce your mindset with uplifting beliefs. *Think and Grow Rich* by Napoleon Hill is a must read, and you can find a free audio version on YouTube.

Where Do You Find Strength?

Intuitively, I will leave you with that question to answer. The inner power that resides in all of us is much greater than we imagine, and I believe things will become better and brighter.

A lot remains to be done to raise human consciousness, and not everyone will leave the world led by ego for one that is driven by the heart.

However, it is my hope that what you have read contributes to sparking your light and enflaming your passion, resulting in you creating a life where self-love, fulfillment, joy, and happiness fill every second of your every day in the life experience your soul has chosen.

May you do a-bun-dance for every victory, big or small, in growing your interest in money, even if ADHD makes it challenging.

Believe that you are enough, worth it, deserving, loved, and supported by something much bigger than you that wants only one thing: an amazing life for you.

All you have to do is to step into your light, embrace your unique brain and all the wonderful things it comes with, think outside the box, be your true self, and make sure to be surrounded by people who love and believe in you. The ones who don't are not worth your time, and you can refuse to let them bring you down.

One final thought I wish to share with you has been of great value to me. It was known to me that the first breath we take when we are born and whether or not we were breastfed (including the quantity of milk we had access to if we were) influences our relationship with money and abundance.

Finding out if your first breath came easily and naturally or not and what you experienced with breastfeeding could say a lot about your struggles.

For example, my mother breastfed me but didn't have enough milk to fulfill my needs. For the longest time, I would make reserves of certain foods, fearing lack of it. As for money, fear of not having enough had been a huge block until I connected these dots.

Learning that abundance is a birthright was a huge aha! At any time, you can reclaim it. I did, and I hope you will too.

Believe and be crazy enough to think that you can make a difference in the world. Whether gigantic or small, make it an everyday thing. Shine your light. Plant seeds of love, hope, compassion, understanding, enlightenment, and gratitude every day without the attachment of any result, because oftentimes you won't see it right away, but have faith that it will work its magic! And once that magic appears, life will be a-bun-dance.

Friendly Reminders for A-Bun-Dance 4 Your Finance

1. Paying attention to what goes on in your body, the physical sensations and emotions as well as the language of your inner critic, is a way resistance shows up as you move from an old way of being to a new one.

2. In any situation, your reaction and what you decide to do with it is what makes the difference between staying in your comfort zone and moving forward.

3. Defense mechanisms are deeply programmed, and the subconscious mind is well trained in reacting a certain way without you even realizing it, keeping you locked inside yourself until you open up your heart to release the pain, hurt, and suffering and break free.

4. Learn and practice saying no to whatever is not aligned with who you really are and what is not true to you. Please yourself before trying to please others.

5. You are enough, and no one should make you think or believe otherwise, because if they do, you have handed over pieces of your inner power. Only what you think and believe about yourself matters.

6. You are here to shine, sparkle, glow, be who you truly and genuinely are, and live your life according to what your soul wants to accomplish.

7. Building a money and energy reserve helps with envisioning what it would be like to actually have money saved up and plenty of energy to enjoy life fully.

8. Always be present and aware of how your ADHD challenges show up, and pause to get a better understanding of what's going on *before* you get discouraged and give up.

Igniting the Spark

- Reassess your relationship with money to get a clear perspective on how far you've come since you started this work. Use these questions to journal on your experience so far.

    - How has your relationship with money evolved and transformed since you started this journey?
    - What progress have you made toward the improvement you chose to work on in chapter 1 because your relationship with money is different?

- Wake up every day, expressing your gratitude for three things, and repeat every night before going to bed. Your brain will cultivate a positive vibration during the night.

- Remember: you have freedom of choice or free will, which means what you choose is not externally determined. When you connect to your heart, this sacred space within where peace and harmony live, where you know you are worthy and whole, the powerful energy and light you are, brings forth your light and lets it shine in a magnificent spectrum of sparkles.

- When something great and awesome happens, thank the Universe for helping you and ask for more. You can even ask the Universe to show you how it can be better than this in the future.

Ready to set your genius on fire and live in alignment with your sparkling energy?

Visit www.indigo.coach and discover all the possibilities available to you in the unique approach Zarina Boily created to facilitate your life experience with ADHD so you can create a fulfilling and empowered life.

Her areas of expertise include:

Using your ADHD creativity to thrive in the world

- Embracing your Sacred Money Archetypes® to deepen financial abundance
- Honoring your difference by recognizing how amazing and wicked it is to be a highly sensitive, free-spirited being
- Bringing in Indigo energy to deepen your understanding of yourself to navigate the world with more ease.
- Reconnecting with your inner child to allow more fun and joy in your life

www.ingramcontent.com/pod-product-compliance
Lightning Source LLC
Chambersburg PA
CBHW020651220526
45464CB00001B/391